CW00547414

Edexcel
GCSE PE
Personal Exercise
Programme

Student Companion

Ray Shaw and Matthew Penny

Illuminate
Publishing

Endorsement Statement

In order to ensure that this resource offers high-quality support for the associated Pearson qualification, it has been through a review process by the awarding body. This process confirms that this resource fully covers the teaching and learning content of the specification or part of a specification at which it is aimed. It also confirms that it demonstrates an appropriate balance between the development of subject skills, knowledge and understanding, in addition to preparation for assessment.

Endorsement does not cover any guidance on assessment activities or processes (e.g. practice questions or advice on how to answer assessment questions), included in the resource nor does it prescribe any particular approach to the teaching or delivery of a related course.

While the publishers have made every attempt to ensure that advice on the qualification and its assessment is accurate, the official specification and associated assessment guidance materials are the only authoritative source of information and should always be referred to for definitive guidance.

Pearson examiners have not contributed to any sections in this resource relevant to examination papers for which they have responsibility.

Examiners will not use endorsed resources as a source of material for any assessment set by Pearson. Endorsement of a resource does not mean that the resource is required to achieve this Pearson qualification, nor does it mean that it is the only suitable material available to support the qualification, and any resource lists produced by the awarding body shall include this and other appropriate resources.

Published in 2021 by Illuminate Publishing Limited, an imprint of Hodder Education, an Hachette UK Company, Carmelite House, 50 Victoria Embankment, London EC4Y 0DZ

Orders: Please visit www.illuminatepublishing.com or email sales@illuminatepublishing.com

© Ray Shaw and Matthew Penny

The moral rights of the author have been asserted.

All rights reserved. No part of this book may be reprinted, reproduced or utilised in any form or by any electronic, mechanical, or other means, now known or hereafter invented, including photocopying and recording, or in any information storage and retrieval system, without permission in writing from the publishers.

British Library Cataloguing in Publication Data

A catalogue record for this book is available from the British Library

ISBN 978-1-913963-05-7

10.22

Printed by Ashford Colour Press, UK

The publisher's policy is to use papers that are natural, renewable and recyclable products made from wood grown in sustainable forests. The logging and manufacturing processes are expected to conform to the environmental regulations of the country of origin.

Every effort has been made to contact copyright holders of material reproduced in this book. If notified, the publishers will be pleased to rectify any errors or omissions at the earliest opportunity.

Editor: Haremi Ltd.
Design: John Dickinson Graphic Design
Cover design: Neil Sutton Cambridge Design Consultants

Typeset by York Publishing Solutions Pvt Ltd, India
Cover photograph: © Rocksweeper / Shutterstock.com

Acknowledgements

(Edexcel GCSE PE specification) Pearson Edexcel (Issue 3 2020) 'GCSE (9-1) Physical Eduction' London, Pearson Education Limited. pp. 4, 21–23, 35, 36, 47. Available at https://qualifications.pearson.com/en/qualifications/edexcel-gcses/physical-education-2016.html; (12-minute Cooper run) Cooper, K. H. (1968) 'A Means of Assessing Maximal Oxygen Intake', JAMA. 203, p. 135–138, in Brian Mackenzie (n.d.) BrianMac Sports Coach. Available at https://www.brianmac.co.uk/; (Abdominal sit-up test, Hand grip strength test, Sit and reach, Illinois agility run test, 30 m sprint test, Vertical jump, Ruler drop) Davis, B. et al. (2000) 'Physical Education and the Study of Sport' 4th edn, London, Harcourt Publishers, copyright Elsevier. pp. 123, 124, 125, 129, 130; (Alternate hand wall throw) Beashal, P. and Taylor, J. (1997) 'The World of Sport Examined', Croatia, Thomas Nelson and Sons, p. 66 in Brian Mackenzie (n.d.) BrianMac Sports Coach. Available at https://www.brianmac.co.uk/; (Harvard step test) Beashal, P. and Taylor, J. (1997) 'The World of Sport Examined', Croatia, Thomas Nelson and Sons, p. 55 in Brian Mackenzie (n.d.) BrianMac Sports Coach. Available at https://www.brianmac.co.uk/havard.htm; (Multi-stage fitness test) Bizley, K. et al. (2012) 'BTEC First Sport Level 2', London, Harper Collins Publishers Limited, p. 303, Figure 3, in Brian Mackenzie (n.d.) BrianMac Sports Coach. Available at https://www.brianmac.co.uk/; (One-minute press-up test) Golding et al. (1986) 'Y's Way to Physical Fitness: The Complete Guide to Fitness Testing and Instruction', 3rd edn, USA, Human Kinetics, in Brian Mackenzie (n.d.) BrianMac Sports Coach [Online]. Available at https://www.brianmac.co.uk/; (Standing broad jump) Hede, C. et al. (2011) 'PE Senior Physical Education for Queensland' Oxford, Oxford University Press. p. 178–179, in Brian Mackenzie (n.d.) BrianMac Sports Coach. Available at https://www.brianmac.co.uk/; (Stand stork test) Johnson, B.L. and Nelson, J.K. (1979) 'Practical Measurements for Evaluation in Physical Education' 4th edn, Minneapolis, Burgess in Brian Mackenzie (n.d.) BrianMac Sports Coach. Available at https://www.brianmac.co.uk/; (Wallsit) Topend Sports (n.d.) 'Single-Leg Wall Sit Test' Topend Sports [Online]. Available at https://www.topendsports.com/testing/tests/wall-sit.htm (Accessed 10 December 2020).

Photographs

p.10 (wheelchair basketball) ACHPF / Shutterstock.com; p.10 (doubles tennis) sirtravelalot / Shutterstock.com; p.11 (ankle injury) comzeal images / Shutterstock.com; p. 11 (man thinking) Master1305 / Shutterstock; p.13 (netballer) Alex Bogatyrev / Shutterstock.com; p.17 (netball game) Alex Bogatyrev / Shutterstock.com; p.21 (cyclists) Suzanne Tucker / Shutterstock.com; p.22 (wicket keeper) ChrisVanLennepPhoto / Shutterstock.com; p.26 (blood pressure monitor) Lesterman / Shutterstock.com; p.27 (wrist) caimacanul / Shutterstock.com; p.27 (neck) LeventeGyori / Shutterstock.com; p.29 (netball game) Juice Flair / Shutterstock.com; p.40 (target) peterschreiber.media / Shutterstock.com; p.41 (coach and player) Rawpixel.com / Shutterstock.com; p.44 (400 metres) Natursports / Shutterstock.com; p.52 (rugby) Paolo Bona / Shutterstock.com; p.53 (plan and equipment) Prostock-studio / Shutterstock.com; p.54 (rugby silhouette) Snap2Art / Shutterstock.com; p.58 (box jumps) Daxiao Productions / Shutterstock.com; p.62 (notepad) Andrei Kuzmik / Shutterstock.com; p.63 (rugby player) OSTILL is Franck Camhi / Shutterstock.com; p.77/78 (golfer) Black Creator 24 / Shutterstock.com; p.81 (hockey player) Studio77 FX vector / Shutterstock.com; p. 85 (graph) WR36 / Shutterstock.com; p.86 (footballer) leolintang / Shutterstock.com; p.88 (swimmer silhouette) Black Creator 24 / Shutterstock.com; p.96 (dancers) Iakov Filimonov / Shutterstock.com; p.97 (basketball) ShutterOK / Shutterstock.com; p.97 (swimmer) Jacob Lund / Shutterstock.com.

Please note: The specification information in this book is correct at the time of going to press. It is, however, important to check with your examination board (Edexcel) to view their current specification and assessment information.

Contents

How to use this book

This book has been specifically written for the non-exam assessment (NEA) component of the Edexcel GCSE Physical Education Personal Exercise Programme (PEP). You must make sure that before starting any work on your programme you check with your awarding body to ensure you are working to the very latest and most up-to-date version of their specification. Updates or alterations to the specification are always clearly available on the Edexcel website.

What is a PEP?

Bold is used throughout this book to highlight important information that will help you develop your PEP.

A PEP is a **personal exercise programme** which you (the student) will design to help improve performance in one chosen practical activity from the list provided in Component 3: Practical Performance (see Appendix 2, p. 105, for the **activity list** to choose from). This be may either one of the three activities you decide to be tested on for Component 3, or another activity from that list.

How will you complete your PEP?

You must carry out your chosen method of training over six to eight weeks.

Your teachers should ensure that your personal exercise programme enables you to:
- draw on appropriate **theory**
- collect, analyse and present **data**.

The use of theory and data are assessed as part of the personal exercise programme aspect of the chosen activity.

This book will take you through step-by-step, providing you with examples of what to include, and opportunities to write in different sections as you develop your PEP. This will become a very useful draft to use when writing your final verbal or written presentation.

You can use the **checklist** in Appendix 1, p. 104, as your **success criteria** to aim towards when you work through your PEP. Your PEP will need to meet the objectives detailed on pages 6–7 and you will be assessed against the assessment criteria.

For the teachers

Always make sure that you're working with the most current version of the specification. Check with the awarding body before starting students on any programme planning. The most recent guidance for teachers will be found on the awarding body website, where you can view and download any updates or amendments: https://qualifications.pearson.com/en/qualifications/edexcel-gcses/physical-education-2016.html

How the book is organised

The book is designed to support you in the planning of your personal exercise programme. Each chapter within the book offers guidance on PEP preparation and makes links to the written examination element of the course. You can write in various sections to help you develop your PEP.

These are the key features that will help you make the most of this book:

What to do and why

This describes what you will do and why it is important.

How to do it

This gives step-by-step instructions for you to follow as you work through your PEP.

Example

This shows a sample of what the presentation of your work could look like. Each chapter will be linked to specific sports.

Have a go!

This gives an explanation of the work needed and is an opportunity for you to record your responses and develop your PEP.

Exam-style questions

Exam-style questions are included in each chapter to help you connect with the written exam as you do the practical work. You have space to complete these in the book if you wish.

Sample answers are included in Appendix 3, p. 108, which you can use to mark your own answers or those of your peers.

Revisit, reflect, revise!

Challenge tasks are included in each chapter, where you have an opportunity to reflect on your work and amend it as you link it to top-level assessment objectives.

Level descriptors

Assessment criteria, specific to each assessment objective, are provided to help you check your progress as you develop your PEP.

Hints and tips

Helpful advice is given as you work through each chapter.

Links to key areas of study

This is where you will find links to the key areas of study:

Component 1: Fitness and Body Systems

 Topic 1: Applied anatomy and physiology

Topic 2: Movement analysis

Topic 3: Physical training

Topic 4: Use of data

Component 2: Health and Performance

Topic 1: Health, fitness and wellbeing

Topic 2: Sports psychology

Topic 3: Socio-cultural influences

Topic 4: Use of data

Key words

The important words are highlighted in the main text and listed at the end of each chapter; they will help you apply the theory (and help with your revision for the written exams). They are also given in the Glossary, p. 101, with definitions.

Example

Have a go!

Completing this task may help your decision

My individual activity:

Pros: ....

Exam-style questions

1. Identify one factor that affects participation levels. (1)

....

2. Describe a personal or event experience that has influence participation in an activity. (1)

revisit ◀ reflect ▶ revise!

- **Revisit** the work completed so far in your personal exercise prog
- Using Figure 3.3 on the next page to **reflect** on your 'initial analy you have compared data against national norms.
- **Revise** any key words and look over the health, fitness and wellb area in your own notes to help you produce a detailed analysis.

WHAT'S MY LEVEL?

Edexcel: level descriptors for initial analysi

Level 1	Level 2	Level 3	Level 4
Limited or little interpretation of	Some attempt at interpretation	Good interpretation and analysis of	Very good interpretation

Hints and tips

- Make sure you have taken time to think about your chosen activity.

Links to key areas

Below are recommended links to **Components 1** and **2**. notes and apply to your PEP.

Component 1: Fitness and Body Systems

Topic 3: Physical training (3.1 & 3.2)

KEYWORDS

Adaptable	Controlled
Aesthetic	Efficient
Confident	Technical

Edexcel

Content

The following content areas from the Edexcel specification are covered in this book:

- aim and planning analysis
- carrying out and monitoring the PEP
- evaluation of PEP.

Edexcel objectives

The following objectives have been paraphrased and restructured from the Edexcel GCSE (9–1) Physical Education specification document:

1. Initial analysis – Interpretation and analysis of pre-PEP fitness tests and sporting/activity performance
2. Initial evaluation – Evaluation and justification of method(s) of training, SMART targets and principles of training
3. Post-PEP analysis – Fitness test results are compared and interpreted
4. Post-PEP evaluation – Evaluation of the overall effectiveness of your PEP in improving performance, including evaluation of the application of the method of training, SMART targets and principles of training with justified future recommendations
5. Overall coherence and structure – Use of appropriate terminology.

Edexcel assessment criteria

- Total of 20 marks
- This is worth 10% of the final grade.

Task: Students are required to select one physical activity and sport on which to plan a personal exercise programme with the intention of improving their performance in that activity.

	Level 1 (1–4 marks)	Level 2 (5–8 marks)	Level 3 (9–12 marks)	Level 4 (13–16 marks)	Level 5 (17–20 marks)
Initial analysis	Limited or little interpretation of fitness test results using some data.	Some attempt at interpretation and analysis of fitness test results using some data, but with errors that may impact analysis.	Good interpretation and analysis of fitness test results using appropriate data, with some errors that have insignificant impact on the analysis.	Very good interpretation and analysis of fitness test results using appropriate data, with one or two minor errors not significantly affecting the analysis.	Excellent and thorough interpretation and analysis of fitness test results using appropriate data.
Initial evaluation	Limited evaluation (mainly descriptive) resulting in inappropriate selection of training method(s) and little application of SMART targets and principles of training to meet performance goal(s).	Some attempts at evaluation, with weak justification for training method(s) chosen, and attempts at applying SMART targets and principles of training to meet performance goal(s), with errors of judgement affecting the quality of the evaluation.	Good evaluation with appropriate training method(s) selected and explained, and application of SMART targets and principles of training to meet performance goal(s), with some errors of judgement that have insignificant impact on the evaluation.	Evaluation with appropriate training method(s) selected and explained, and application of SMART targets and principles of training to meet performance goal(s), with few errors of judgement not significantly affecting the evaluation.	Evaluation with appropriate training method(s) selected and justified, and application of SMART targets and principles of training to meet performance goal(s).

	Level 1 (1–4 marks)	Level 2 (5–8 marks)	Level 3 (9–12 marks)	Level 4 (13–16 marks)	Level 5 (17–20 marks)
Post-PEP analysis	Limited comparison, interpretation and/or analysis of differences and/or similarities between fitness test results and little/no supporting evidence used, with many significant errors of judgement/inaccuracies.	Attempts to compare and interpret the fitness test results, with some differences and/or similarities analysed in places and some supporting evidence used, but with many errors of judgement/inaccuracies.	Fitness test results are compared and interpreted, and the differences and/or similarities are analysed and sufficient supporting evidence used, but with some errors of judgement/inaccuracies.	Fitness test results are compared and interpreted, and the differences and/or similarities are analysed with satisfactory supporting evidence, but with some minor errors of judgment/inaccuracies.	Fitness tests results are compared and interpreted, and the differences and/or similarities identified and analysed, and reasons for them justified, with ample supporting evidence.
Post-PEP evaluation	Limited evaluation of the application of the method(s) of training, SMART goals and principles of training, and no recommendation for improving future training and performance.	Some attempts at evaluation of the application of the method(s) of training, SMART goals and principles of training, with some attempt at recommendation for improving future training and performance, but with significant errors.	Good evaluation of the application of the method(s) of training, SMART goals and principles of training, with sufficient detail/depth, and appropriate recommendation(s) to improve future training and performance.	Well-argued evaluation of the application of the method(s) of training, SMART goals and principles of training, in satisfactory detail and depth, with justified recommendations to improve future training and performance.	Sophisticated evaluation of the application of the method(s) of training, SMART goals and principles of training, in good detail and depth, with well justified recommendations to improve future training and performance.
Overall coherence and conciseness of the student's PEP	Lack of coherence and structure, with inappropriate and inaccurate terminology throughout.	Attempts at coherence and structure, with use of appropriate terminology in places but inconsistent and with some errors of judgement.	Good coherence and structure, with appropriate terminology used, but some errors of judgement/accuracy with no significant impact on the piece.	Very good coherence and structure, with appropriate terminology used throughout, but with a few minor errors.	Excellent coherence and structure, with appropriate terminology used consistently, with few minor, if any, errors.

Choosing your activity

You will be assessed in *three* different physical activities as a *performer* in Component 3: Practical Performance in:

- at least *one* activity as an individual performer
- *one* activity within a team sport
- *one* other activity of your choice from the approved activities lists.

You can choose *one* of these on which to plan your PEP or you may choose another activity from the activity list in Component 3: Practical Performance. This can be either a team activity or an individual activity. Once you have decided upon your activity, you can start to design a 'personal exercise programme' (PEP). Note: This may also be called a 'personal *training* programme'.

By the end of this chapter:

- you will be able to choose your activity so that you can begin to plan your PEP.

What to do and why

- You will design a personal exercise programme which will help to improve **fitness** and more importantly, performance in your **chosen** activity.
- From your **practical profile** choose *one* activity to be your **chosen activity** to be linked to your PEP. You also have the option of picking an activity that is not one of the three practical activities you have selected.

> Check the latest specification online for updates.

How to do it

The following activity list has been taken from the Edexcel specification. Choose one activity from the list to form your practical profile.

Table 1.1 Edexcel GCSE Physical Education activity list

> Edexcel

Team activities	
Activity	**Forbidden combinations and rules**
Acrobatic gymnastics*	
Association football	Cannot be five-a-side
Badminton	Cannot be assessed with singles/individual activity badminton
Basketball	Cannot be 'street basketball'
Camogie	Cannot be assessed with hurling
Cricket	
Dance	Acceptable dances include: ballet, ballroom, contemporary/modern, cultural (includes hip-hop, Irish, Indian, jazz, Latin), folk and street This can only be used for one activity

Team activities	
Activity	**Forbidden combinations and rules**
Field hockey	
Figure skating*	
Futsal*	
Gaelic football	
Handball	
Hurling	Cannot be assessed with camogie
Ice hockey*	
Inline/Roller hockey*	
Lacrosse	
Netball	
Rowing	Cannot be assessed with sculling, canoeing, kayaking or a rowing machine. This can only be used for one activity
Rugby league	Cannot be assessed with rugby union or rugby sevens; cannot be tag rugby
Rugby union	Can be assessed as sevens or fifteen-a-side. Cannot be assessed with rugby league; cannot be tag rugby. This can only be used for one activity
Sailing*	Cannot be assessed with singles/individual activity sailing. Royal Yachting Association recognised sailing-boat classes only. Students must perform as helmsman
Sculling*	Cannot be assessed with canoeing, kayaking or rowing
Squash	Cannot be assessed with singles/individual activity squash
Table tennis	Cannot be assessed with singles/individual activity table tennis
Tennis	Cannot be assessed with singles/individual activity tennis
Volleyball	
Water polo*	

Specialist activity**	
Blind cricket	
Goalball	
Powerchair football	
Table cricket	
Wheelchair basketball	
Wheelchair rugby	

Individual activities	
Activity	**Forbidden combinations and rules**
Amateur boxing	
Athletics	Can be assessed in one event from the disciplines of either Track or Field (including cross country*) Race walking is not a permitted Athletics event
Badminton	Cannot be assessed with doubles
BMX cycling*	Racing only, not tricks
Canoeing	Cannot be assessed with kayaking, rowing or sculling
Cycling	Track or road cycling
Dance	This can only be used for one activity
Diving	Platform diving
Figure skating*	

Individual activities	
Activity	**Forbidden combinations and rules**
Golf	
Gymnastics	Floor routines and apparatus
Equestrian	Can be assessed in either show jumping, cross country or dressage
Kayaking	Cannot be assessed with canoeing, rowing or sculling
Rock climbing	Can be indoor or outdoor
Sailing*	Cannot be assessed with sailing as a team activity. Royal Yachting Association recognised sailing-boat classes only
Sculling	Cannot be assessed with rowing, canoeing or kayaking
Skiing	Outdoor/indoor on snow. Cannot be assessed with snowboarding. Must not be on dry slopes
Snowboarding	Outdoor/indoor on snow. Cannot be assessed with skiing. Must not be on dry slopes
Squash	Cannot be assessed with doubles
Swimming	Not synchronised swimming
Table tennis	Cannot be assessed with doubles
Tennis	Cannot be assessed with doubles
Trampolining	
Windsurfing*	
Specialist activity**	
Boccia	
Polybat	

*These activities are available for first teaching from September 2020 and first certification from Summer 2022.

**The specialist activities are available only to those students with a physical disability, and in line with entry criteria set out by that activity's National Governing Body. If a student is classified as eligible, then they should be assessed in the classification based on the relevant activity's National Governing Body classification criteria.

Wheelchair basketball game

Mixed doubles tennis

> Writing is well structured with accurate use of spelling, punctuation and grammar.

Things to think about when choosing your activity

Your activity does *not* have to be your strongest and you will not be assessed on whether or not improvements have occurred to your performance through your training programme, but you *will be* assessed on the following:

Edexcel objectives (adapted from the GCSE (9–1) Physical Education specification)

1. Initial analysis – **Interpretation** and **analysis** of pre-PEP fitness tests and sporting/activity performance

2. Initial evaluation – **Evaluation** and **justification** of method(s) of training, SMART targets and principles of training

3. Post-PEP analysis – Fitness test results are **compared** and **interpreted**

4. Post-PEP evaluation – **Evaluation** of the overall effectiveness of your PEP in improving performance, including evaluation of the application of the method of training, SMART targets and principles of training with **justified** future recommendations

5. Overall coherence and structure – Use of **appropriate** terminology.

See p. 6–7 for the Edexcel assessment criteria.

Questions to ask yourself

Think about these questions when choosing your activity. You should spend time exploring the pros and cons for each activity and record your notes in your practical profile.

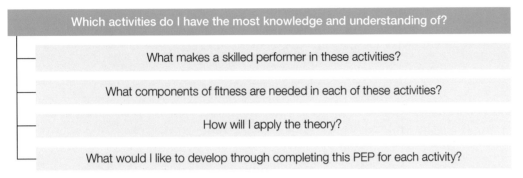

Which activities do I have the most knowledge and understanding of?

What makes a skilled performer in these activities?

What components of fitness are needed in each of these activities?

How will I apply the theory?

What would I like to develop through completing this PEP for each activity?

Figure 1.1 Strongest and weakest activity

What do I know about my injury?

Have I been given a rehabilitation plan?

Yes – This will give me a focus to help motivate myself through my rehabilitation.

No – I need to seek medical advice before starting a rehabilitation plan.

The data I collect may be limited depending upon the injury sustained.

Figure 1.2 Rehabilitation from an injury

How can I recover from an injury?

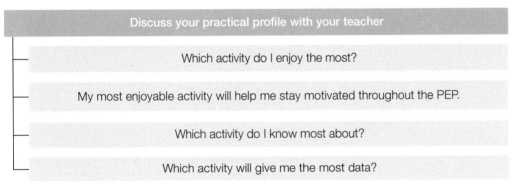

Discuss your practical profile with your teacher

Which activity do I enjoy the most?

My most enjoyable activity will help me stay motivated throughout the PEP.

Which activity do I know most about?

Which activity will give me the most data?

Figure 1.3 What to do if uncertain

Hmm, what are my strongest and weakest activities?

What can I do to overcome my injury?

Help! I just don't know what to choose! What do I do?

Have a go!

Completing this task may help your decision-making process.

My individual activity:

Pros: ....

....

Cons: ....

....

My team activity:

Pros: ....

....

Cons: ....

....

The activity of my choice:

Pros: ....

....

Cons: ....

....

> 'Pros' are the **advantages** and 'cons' are the **disadvantages**.

You can explore the **characteristics** of a **skilled performer** in your activity as well as the major **components of fitness** needed. Producing a plan like this will help you when you come to think about targets later on.

Note: This may form part of your written introduction.

Example: Characteristics of a netball player

Making connections

There will be links between characteristics and the components of fitness as shown by the arrows in Figure 1.4, e.g. to be **controlled** within a game of netball you will need a good level of **balance** and **coordination**.

To be effective as a centre in netball you may decide that cardiovascular fitness, **speed** and coordination are the top three components of fitness needed (as indicated by the stars in Figure 1.4).

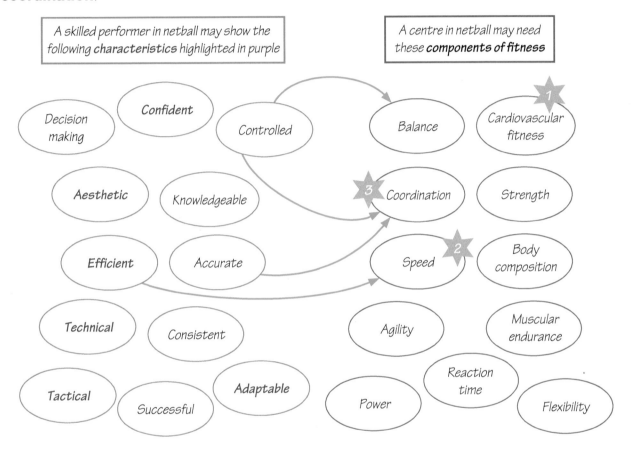

Figure 1.4 Linking characteristics and components of fitness

You can use Figure 1.4 to apply characteristics and components of fitness to examples within the game, for example:

As a centre in netball, I will need a good level of coordination within a game to produce controlled movements, such as catching and passing in one efficient movement to move the ball away from a defender.

Have a go!

Complete Figure 1.5 below:

1. Add your chosen activity to the centre of your diagram. Identify the **characteristics** needed for a skilled performer in this activity (using the space on the left in green).
2. Identify the **components of fitness** needed to perform in your chosen activity (using the space on the right in red).
3. Once you have done this, **rank order** them in terms of which ones you feel are most important.

> To 'rank order' means putting things in order of importance, e.g. 1st, 2nd.

A skilled performer in .... may show the following **characteristics.**

A .... may need the following **components of fitness.**

Figure 1.5 Identifying characteristics and components of fitness

Making connections

● Which components of fitness will help you improve a specific characteristic?

....

....

....

....

....

....

● Identify the main components involved in your activity:

....

....

....

....

....

....

● Give examples of characteristics, components of fitness and application to your chosen activity:

....

....

....

....

....

....

These connections can be made throughout the PEP and you may like to start with applying some of these within your introduction.

Exam-style questions

1. Identify one factor that has an impact on participation levels. (1)

....

2. Describe a personal or event experience that has influenced your participation in an activity. (1)

....

3. Identify **four** characteristics of a skilled performer. (4)

....

....

4. State **four** components of fitness for a skilled performer. (4)

....

....

....

....

KEYWORDS

Adaptable
Aesthetic
Balance
Characteristics
Confident
Controlled
Coordination
Efficient
Skilled performer
Speed
Tactical
Technical

The definitions are given in the Glossary, p. 101.

Hints and tips

- Make sure you have taken time to think about your chosen activity. Is it on the activity list for Edexcel?
- Know the components of fitness required for your activity and the ones specific to your position or event.
- Explore the characteristics that will help improve your performance and explore their connections to components of fitness.

Links to key areas

Below are recommended links to **Components 1** and **2**. Look over your class notes and apply to your PEP.

Component 1: Fitness and Body Systems

 Topic 3: Physical training (3.1 & 3.2)

Component 2: Health and Performance

 Topic 1: Health, fitness and wellbeing (1.1)

 Topic 3: Socio-cultural influences (3.1)

Your introduction

Once you have decided upon your activity, a good way to begin your PEP is to explain a bit about your background, how you became interested in the sport and what your performance **goals** are. This will form the introduction to your PEP.

By the end of this chapter:

● you will have started to think about the introduction to your PEP.

What to do and why?

Although there is no assessment objective linked directly to your **introduction**, this is an opportunity to show some application to theory (see **Links to key areas** at the end of this chapter, p. 20). It's important to remember this focus whilst writing your PEP and to keep your introduction as short as possible due to the overall word limit of 1500 words; don't forget you can place supplementary information in an appendix to support your writing.

Introduce your PEP so the reader (teacher/moderator) can gather some **background information** on your chosen activity and your performance aims.

How to do it

In your introduction you could write about:

● the sport/physical activity you are involved in
● the events/matches you are taking part in
● the position you play (team sport)
● how often you train and take part in competition sport
● your strengths and weaknesses in one aspect of your sport or activity
● your goals and **motivation**.

You could choose netball as your activity

> Bella is making connections here between **components** of speed, flexibility and agility and **characteristics** of **fluency** and **control** needed for the game.

Introduction
My practical profile

Name: Bella Mae   **Gender:** Female   **Age:** 15

Chosen activity: Netball   **Position:** Centre

Activity	Individual/team
Netball	Team

My chosen activity will be netball.

I am captain of the school team and play in the centre position. My strengths are my **speed, flexibility and agility** as I'm quick to get into space and I can change direction quickly to get away from defenders. These components allow me to be fluent and controlled on court.

Although I train 2 times every week, I think my **cardiovascular fitness** could be improved as I tend to get tired towards the end of games and this reduces my impact on the play.

My main goal is to play for Wales U17s, and I'm hoping to be selected for trials at the end of this season.

Have a go!

Now you have seen an example introduction for a netball player and know and understand the information you need to include, you are ready to write a **draft** introduction about yourself. Due to the maximum number of words you can submit for your PEP (1500) keep your introduction as short as possible; you can always add supplementary information to an appendix if you need to. You could use a similar approach to this one to help you structure the information you're likely to need:

A 'draft' means it is an early attempt that you can change later.

Note: You may want to change this later as you work your way through your PEP.

Introduction
My practical profile

Name: Gender: Age:

Chosen activity: Position:

Activity	Individual/team

....

....

....

....

....

Exam-style questions

As there are no assessment objectives linked directly to your introduction, there are no related exam questions.

Hints and tips

Tick ✔ this checklist when you have included it in your introduction:

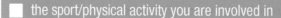

- [ ] the sport/physical activity you are involved in
- [ ] the events/matches you are taking part in
- [ ] the position you play (team sport)
- [ ] your strengths and weaknesses in one aspect of your sport or activity
- [ ] your goals or motivation.

KEY WORDS

Agility
Cardiovascular fitness
Characteristics
Components of fitness
Control
Fitness
Flexibility
Fluency
Goals
Motivation
Speed

Links to key areas

Below are recommended links to **Components 1** and **2**. Look over your class notes and apply to your PEP.

Component 1: Fitness and Body Systems

 Topic 1: Applied anatomy and physiology (1.4)

 Topic 3: Physical training (3.3 & 3.4)

Component 2: Health and Performance

 Topic 1: Health, fitness and wellbeing (1.1 & 1.2)

 Topic 3: Socio-cultural influences (3.1)

Initial analysis

Before you design your PEP you will need an understanding of your personal strengths and weaknesses. You will need an understanding of these to identify targets that you can work on to bring about improvements in your performance.

By the end of this chapter:

- you will know your strengths and weaknesses in your chosen sport
- you will begin to think about targets for improvement.

What to do and why

You will need to think carefully about your chosen sport or activity and identify the **components of fitness** required to perform effectively and efficiently. For example, a centre in netball may require **cardiovascular fitness, agility** and **speed** to perform effectively in a game of netball.

To find out your strengths and weaknesses, you will need to complete a range of fitness tests for the components of fitness specific to your sport or activity. Once you have collected the data complete an initial analysis by comparing your fitness against **national norms**.

How to do it

There are 11 components of fitness that are present in your everyday life (see Table 3.1). These are elements of exercise and fitness specific to your needs and the demands of your chosen sport or activity. Before you can complete your initial analysis you will need an understanding of:

- the **components of fitness** and their definitions
- how each component is used within sports and activities
- **test protocols** for each component of fitness.

Application of components of fitness

You need a good knowledge and understanding of the components of fitness as well as their definitions. Once you have this understanding you should then be able to apply specific examples to your chosen activity.

Cyclists need good muscular endurance as they use their muscles continuously throughout a race

A wicket keeper needs a good reaction time as they have to dive to catch a ball coming off the batsman

Use Table 3.1 to help you develop your knowledge and understanding of the components of fitness.

Table 3.1   Components of fitness

Component	Definition	Example
Muscle endurance	Where a specific muscle group is exercised repeatedly over a period of time	A cyclist using the muscles in her legs continuously throughout the **duration** of the race
Cardiovascular fitness	The ability to exercise for a sustained period of time	A midfield player in football playing at the same **intensity** for the full duration of the match
Strength	The maximum force a muscle can generate against a resistance	A prop forward in rugby pushing against his opponent as the ball comes into the scrum
Flexibility	The range of movement at a joint	A gymnast performing the splits in a beam routine
Body composition	The percentage of body weight that is fat, muscle and bone	A 100 m sprinter would require more muscle mass than a marathon runner. Both would have reduced body fat as it would impact their performance
Agility	The ability to change direction at speed	A squash player would need to change direction at speed on court to return a shot
Speed	The time taken to get from A to B as quickly as possible	A 100 m sprinter moving from the start line to the finish line as fast as possible
Power	Strength × speed	A shot putter moving the arm rapidly forward to propel the shot through the air
Coordination	The ability to move two or more body parts at the same time	A tennis player throwing the ball up with one hand, then using the other hand to strike the ball with the racket to perform a serve
Balance	Stability of the body's centre of mass over a base of support	A gymnast performing a handstand
Reaction time	Time taken to respond to a stimulus	A wicket keeper in cricket diving to catch the ball coming off the bat of the batsman

Test protocols for each component of fitness

It is important to follow test **protocols** for **reliability** and **validity** purposes. You will see that some components of fitness have a number of different tests, e.g. 'strength' has the grip dynamometer test and 1 rep max test (as shown in Table 3.2). It is important to choose the test that is specific to your needs.

Table 3.2 provides a summary of fitness test protocols that will help you develop your knowledge and understanding. You should, however, visit the recommended websites for a full list of test protocols.

https://brianmac.co.uk/   https://www.topendsports.com/

> You will have seen the terms 'reliability' and 'validity' in your science work.

> This is not an extensive list of tests but it is a summary of protocols. Further reading is recommended.

Table 3.2 Fitness tests and protocols

Component of fitness	Fitness test	Protocol
Cardiovascular fitness (aerobic endurance)	Multi-stage fitness test	• Stay in time with the bleeps on each line on a 20 m course. • Run until exhaustion prevents completion of three consecutive **shuttles**.
	Cooper's 12-minute run	• Record the distance covered in 12 minutes.
	Cooper's 12-minute swim test	• Record the number of lengths/distance covered in 12 minutes.
	Harvard step test	• Step up and down off a 45 cm high gym bench for 5 minutes at a rate 30 steps/minute.
Strength	Grip dynamometer	• Grip with dominant hand. • Apply **maximal force**. • Repeat three times and record the maximal force.
	1 rep max	• Warm up with a light weight. • Provide a one-minute rest period. • Choose a weight that is achievable. • Rest for one minute. • Continue the sequence, progressively adding weight until **failure**.
Muscular endurance	1 minute sit-up / press-up test	• Perform as many full sit-ups / press-ups as you can in 60 seconds.
	Wall sit	• Sit with your back supported against a wall and your knees bent to 90 degrees. Hold that position for as long as you can.
Flexibility	Sit and reach test	• Remove shoes and place feet up against the box. • Keep knees locked and reach over the box. • Stretch and hold the position for two seconds recording the distance reached.
Body composition	Skinfold callipers	• Take four measurements: biceps, **triceps**, back and hip. • Convert readings to body-fat percentage.
Agility	Illinois agility run test	• Start lying face-down on the start line. • Complete the course, following the exact distances and record the time taken.
Balance	Standing stork test	• Place hands on hips and one foot on the opposing knee of the other leg. • Raise heel and hold balance for as long as possible.
Coordination	Alternate hand wall throw	• Stand two metres from a smooth-surfaced wall. • Throw the ball to the wall with one hand and catch with the other. • Record how many consecutive catches you can make in 30 seconds.
Power	Vertical jump	• Stand sideways against the wall, measure height with an upstretched arm. • Jump up as high as you can and mark the wall. • Measure the distance between the two marks.
	Standing broad jump	• Stand with feet shoulder width apart. • Jump as far as possible and measure the distance.
Reaction time	Ruler drop test	• Hold a 30 cm ruler with the 0 between the thumb and first finger. • Your partner is ready to catch, with a gap between their thumb and first finger. • Drop the ruler with no warning. • Your partner catches the ruler as quickly as possible; record the distance from the top of their thumb.
Speed	30 m sprint	• Sprint 30 m distance. • Timer stands in line with the finish.

Comparing test results to normative data

Many fitness tests have associated data (**normative data** or **national norms**). These norms are very useful for you to use to interpret the test results, but you need to understand what they are and the possible limitations of using them. Table 3.3 gives an example of the national norms for 16-year-old males and females for the multi-stage fitness test.

Table 3.3 Norms for the multi-stage fitness test (cardiovascular fitness)

Gender	Excellent	Above average	Average	Below average	Poor
Boys	L12 / S7	L11 / S2	L8 / S9	L7 / S1	L6 / S6
Girls	L10 / S9	L9 / S1	L6 / S7	L5 / S1	L4 / S7

Bizley, K. et al. (2012) 'BTEC First Sport Level 2' in Brian Mackenzie (n.d.) BrianMac Sports Coach [Online].

When using norms to compare and interpret your test results, you must consider if the data is derived from a test using the same **protocol**. It is not always clear what the test **procedure** is by the name of the test, for example the 'Multi-stage fitness test' can be performed in numerous ways, such as a 15 metre test and a 20 metre test. So norms using one procedure may not be relevant for another.

It is also important to consider if the norms were derived from a subject **population** and **age group** that is similar to your test group. Many tests were developed in a university setting, so university students make up the population group for many test norms. This group may not always reflect the general population (or your group of teenagers or athletes for example).

Look for norms:

- based on a similar age group
- that are up to date
- of local origin if possible (e.g. from the UK).

Other useful tests

There are other methods of testing including **laboratory tests**, which are costly and may not be as available as **field tests**.

Other methods of measuring **health** and fitness are:

- **sport specific** tests
- **Physical Activity Readiness Questionnaires (PARQ)**
- screening methods such as monitoring **blood pressure (BP)**, **heart rate (HR)** and calorie intake.

Physical Activity Readiness Questionnaire (PARQ)

A Physical Activity Readiness Questionnaire, or PARQ, is a method of uncovering health and lifestyle issues prior to taking part in an exercise programme. Coaches use PARQ questionnaires to determine the risks that exercising poses for an individual based on their health history, any symptoms they are displaying, and other risk factors that affect them. The results can also help the coach design a more effective exercise programme for that individual. The questionnaire is short and easy to administer and reveals any family history of illness.

You can find many examples of a PARQ form (see Figure 3.1) or you could devise your own as a class so that it is common to all students within the class or centre (a blank PARQ form can be found in Appendix 4, p. 111). This could be completed at the start of your PEP prior to any engagement in physical activity.

The PARQ will *not* form part of the assessment, but it is an opportunity to:

- provide the reader of your PEP with some **background information**
- use as evidence, if the intensity of your training programme needs to be adapted for any **health reasons**
- **apply theory**.

PEP

PARQ
Physical Activity Readiness Questionnaire

Objective

A Physical Activity Readiness Questionnaire or PARQ is a method of uncovering health and lifestyle issues prior to taking part in an exercise programme.

Guidance

Please answer all questions as accurately as possible.

Personal details

Name: _____

D.O.B.: _____ Age: _____ Height: _____ Weight: _____

Emergency contact number: _____

Emergency contact name: _____

Relationship of contact: _____

Your address: _____

_____

Contact number: _____

Questions

Are you currently under a doctor's care?   YES ☐   NO ☐

If YES explain: _____

When was the last time you had a physical examination? _____

Do you take any medication on a regular basis?   YES ☐   NO ☐

If YES, please list medications and reasons for taking: _____
_____

Have you recently been hospitalised?   YES ☐   NO ☐

If YES explain: _____

Do you smoke?	YES ☐ NO ☐	History of breathing or lung problems?	YES ☐ NO ☐
Are you pregnant?	YES ☐ NO ☐	Increased blood cholesterol?	YES ☐ NO ☐
Do you drink alcohol more than three times a week?	YES ☐ NO ☐	Describe any regular physical activity you take part in:	

Do you have:

History of heart problems, chest pains?   YES ☐   NO ☐

High blood pressure?   YES ☐   NO ☐

All the information is true to the best of my knowledge.   NAME: SIGNATURE:

Figure 3.1 A PARQ form

Blood pressure (BP)

Blood pressure is the force (pressure) exerted by blood against the arterial walls during a cardiac cycle (heartbeat). The cardiac cycle consists of heart muscle contraction (**systole**) and heart muscle relaxation (**diastole**).

There are two measurements when recording blood pressure:

- **Systolic blood pressure**, which is the higher of the two pressure measurements, occurs as the heart muscles contract, pumping blood into the **aorta**.
- **Diastolic blood pressure**, which is when the heart muscles relax, allowing the heart to refill with blood, and is the lowest pressure.

Ideal systolic blood pressure in an adult varies between 90 and 120 mm Hg, and ideal diastolic pressure varies between 60 and 80 mm Hg (see Figure 3.2).

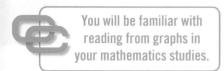

You will be familiar with reading from graphs in your mathematics studies.

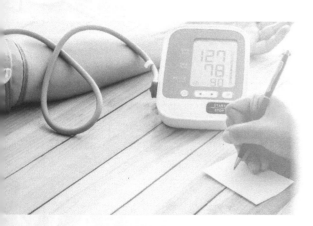

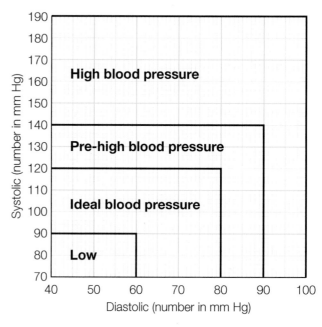

Figure 3.2   A graph showing blood pressure ranges

Heart rate (HR)

Your heart rate is the number of times your heart **beats per minute** (b.p.m.). A normal heart rate is between 60 and 100 b.p.m. while you are resting.

Generally, a *lower resting* heart rate indicates a *higher level* of cardiovascular fitness. The average person has a resting heart rate of between 70 and 75 beats per minute (b.p.m.). Fitter people who take part in lots of aerobic exercise have resting heart rates around 50 and 60 b.p.m. Some professional athletes have resting heart rates as low as the upper 30s!

Calculating HR

You can measure your heart rate at your wrist or your neck:

1. **At your wrist:**
   Lightly press the index and middle fingers of one hand on the opposite wrist, just below the base of the thumb.
2. **At your neck:**
   Lightly press the side of the neck, just below your jawbone.

Count the number of beats in 15 seconds, and multiply by four to give your heart rate per minute.

Calculating maximum heart rate

A quick way to calculate maximum heart rates for different ages is to use this equation:

Maximum heart rate (max HR) = 220 − age

e.g. 220 − 16 = 204 b.p.m.

Heart rate should be measured at the wrist or neck

You will have seen calculations like these in your mathematics studies.

Training zones

A knowledge of heart rates can allow you to train specifically in these **training zones**:

- the **aerobic target zone**, 60% to 80% of your maximum heart rate
- the **anaerobic target zone**, 80% to 90% of your maximum heart rate.

Training in the aerobic target zone will develop your **cardiovascular system**. Your body's ability to transport oxygen to, and carbon dioxide away from, the working muscles can be developed and improved.

Training in the anaerobic target zone will develop your **lactic acid system**. In this zone, your **anaerobic threshold (AT)** is found. This is the point at which your body can no longer remove the lactic acid from the working muscles quickly enough. Through the correct training it is possible to delay the AT by being able to increase your ability to deal with the lactic acid for a longer time, or by pushing the AT higher.

Now you should have a good understanding of:

- the **components of fitness** and their definitions
- how each component is used within sports and activities
- **test protocols** for each component of fitness.

You will have studied aerobic and anaerobic respiration in biology.

Methods of training

Before you start planning a personal exercise plan you will need to have **specific targets** to aim for; there is more help for you to set these targets in Chapter 4. Your training programme can be designed to help improve **fitness** but the main focus will be to improve your **performance** within your chosen activity. One way to identify targets is to identify your strengths and areas for improvement by testing a range of components of fitness. From the data collected you can identify sport-specific areas to focus on to bring about improvements.

Once you have identified your targets, you need to understand **training methods** so that you can develop the component of fitness you have identified. The method of training you choose should match your needs (see Table 3.4). Different methods will need to be used for different people. You will need to apply the **principles of training** to achieve desired results, e.g.

- **continuous** walking for fat loss
- **interval** training to increase speed for a 100 m sprinter.

The principles of training include:

- Individual needs
- Specificity
- Progressive overload
- **FITT (frequency**, intensity, time, type)
- Rest and recovery
- Reversibility
- Thresholds of training (aerobic target zone, 60–80% MHR; anaerobic target zone, 80–90% MHR).

Table 3.4   Different methods of training adapted to suit individual needs

Methods of training	
Continuous	Interval
Fartlek training	Circuit
	Weight/resistance
Walking, running, swimming, cycling, etc.	Interval
	Plyometric

A centre in netball may require a range of components of fitness to perform effectively throughout the duration of a game of netball. Therefore, a netball player may complete fitness tests for all 11 components of fitness (see Table 3.5) to ensure they have an accurate self-analysis. However, a long jumper in athletics may only need to focus on five or six components.

Table 3.5   The 11 components of fitness

Components of fitness	
Agility	Muscular endurance
Balance	Power
Body composition	Reaction time
Cardiovascular fitness (aerobic endurance)	Speed
Coordination	Strength
Flexibility	

A centre in netball may require a range of components of fitness

---

Example

I'm a 15-year-old netball player. I play centre for my local club and my aim this season is to make the hub squad. I have decided to complete the 11 fitness tests, so I can analyse my fitness and then plan my PEP to develop my weaknesses and help me to achieve my goal.

Multi-stage fitness test (Cardiovascular fitness)					

Test result 1: Level 6 Shuttle 7

Gender	Excellent	Above average	Average	Below average	Poor
Boys	L12 / S7	L11 / S2	L8 / S9	L7 / S1	L6 / S6
Girls	L10 / S9	L9 / S1	L6 / S7	L5 / S1	L4 / S7

Bizley, K. et al. (2012) 'BTEC First Sport Level 2' in Brian Mackenzie (n.d.) BrianMac Sports Coach [Online].

Initial analysis

Cardiovascular fitness is an important component of fitness for my position in netball. As a centre in netball I need to cover a large area of the court, as well as being the link between attack and defence. A good level of cardiovascular fitness will allow me to perform effectively for the full duration of the game.

I am disappointed in my score (L6/S7) as it places me as 'Average' when compared to the national norms. I would like to achieve a score of 'Above average'. This is a target area for me to improve so that I can last the full duration of the game.

The student has identified the component of fitness to test.

The student has written about the area she would like to improve.

Have a go!

Now you know more about components of fitness and their application to sporting examples (as well as fitness testing) you are ready to start thinking about completing your initial analysis.

To complete your initial analysis, you must:

1. **Collect data on your current fitness levels.**

   a) Complete a range of fitness tests. Set up each fitness test following the test **protocol** so that the data collected is **valid** and **reliable** (refer to Table 3.2, p. 23).

   b) Record your current levels of fitness. For example, one way to do this could be a simple chart like this one, with space for you to record your results in the first three columns.

Current fitness levels			
Component of fitness	**Fitness test**	**Results**	**Compared to national norm**

2. **Compare with the national norms.**

   a) Compare your test results with the national norms tables below and complete the initial analysis sections.

   b) Record how your current fitness levels compare to the national norms in the Current fitness levels table on page 30 (in the last column).

These will be 'excellent'/'above average'/'average'/'below average'/'poor'.

Note: These tables show norms for a variety of age ranges (between 14–19-year-olds). You can look up other ranges at https://brianmac.co.uk/.

Multi-stage fitness test (Cardiovascular fitness)

Test result 1: Level   Shuttle

Gender	Excellent	Above average	Average	Below average	Poor
Boys	L12 / S7	L11 / S2	L8 / S9	L7 / S1	L6 / S6
Girls	L10 / S9	L9 / S1	L6 / S7	L5 / S1	L4 / S7

Initial analysis

Bizley, K. et al. (2012) 'BTEC First Sport Level 2' in Brian Mackenzie (n.d.) BrianMac Sports Coach [Online].

Cooper's 12-minute run (Cardiovascular fitness)

Test result 1:

Gender	Excellent	Above average	Average	Below average	Poor
Boys	>2800 m	2500–2800 m	2300–2499 m	2200–2299 m	<2200 m
Girls	>2100 m	2000–2100 m	1700–1999 m	1600–1699 m	<1600 m

Initial analysis

Cooper, K.H. (1968) 'A Means of Assessing Maximal Oxygen Intake' in Brian Mackenzie (n.d.) BrianMac Sports Coach [Online].

Harvard step test (Cardiovascular endurance)

Test result 1:

Gender	Excellent	Above average	Average	Below average	Poor
Boys	>90.0	80.0–90.0	65.0–79.9	55.0–64.9	<55.0
Girls	>86.0	76.0–86.0	61.0–75.9	50.0–60.9	<50.0

Initial analysis

Beashel P. & Taylor J. (1997) *The World of Sport Examined*, in Brian Mackenzie (n.d.) BrianMac Sports Coach [Online].

Sit-up test (Muscular endurance)

Test result 1:

Gender	Excellent	Above average	Average	Below average	Poor
Boys	>30	26–30	20–25	17–19	<17
Girls	>25	21–25	15–20	9–14	<9

Initial analysis

This article was published in 'Physical Education and the Study of Sport' 4th edn, Davis, B. et al., p. 124, Copyright Elsevier (2000).

One-minute press-up test (Muscular endurance)

Test result 1:

Gender	Excellent	Good	Above average	Average	Below average	Poor
Boys	>56	47–56	35–46	19–34	11–18	<11
Girls	>35	27–35	21–26	11–20	7–10	<6

Initial analysis

Golding et al. (1986) *Y's Way to Physical Fitness: The Complete Guide to Fitness Testing and Instruction*, in Brian Mackenzie (n.d.) BrianMac Sports Coach [Online].

Grip dynamometer test (grip strength)

Test result 1:

Gender	Excellent	Above average	Average	Below average	Poor
Boys	>56 kg	51–56 kg	45–50 kg	39–44 kg	<39 kg
Girls	>36 kg	31–36 kg	25–30 kg	19–24 kg	<19 kg

Initial analysis

This article was published in 'Physical Education and the Study of Sport' 4th edn, Davis, B. et al., p. 123, Copyright Elsevier (2000).

Sit and reach (Flexibility)

Test result 1:

Gender	Excellent	Above average	Average	Below average	Poor
Boys	>14 cm	14.0–11.0 cm	10.9–7.0 cm	6.9–4.0 cm	<4 cm
Girls	>15 cm	15.0–12.0 cm	11.9–7.0 cm	6.9–4.0 cm	<4 cm

Initial analysis

This article was published in 'Physical Education and the Study of Sport' 4th edn, Davis, B. et al., p. 126, Copyright Elsevier (2000).

Illinois agility run test (Agility)

Test result 1:

Gender	Excellent	Above average	Average	Below average	Poor
Boys	<15.2 s	15.2–16.1 s	16.2–18.1 s	18.2–19.3 s	>19.3 s
Girls	<17.0 s	17.0–17.9 s	18.0–21.7 s	21.8–23.0 s	>23.0 s

Initial analysis

This article was published in 'Physical Education and the Study of Sport' 4th edn, Davis, B. et al., p. 129, Copyright Elsevier (2000).

30 m sprint test (Speed)

Test result 1:

Gender	Excellent	Above average	Average	Below average	Poor
Boys	<4.0 s	4.0–4.2 s	4.3–4.4 s	4.5–4.6 s	>4.6 s
Girls	<4.5 s	4.5–4.6 s	4.7–4.8 s	4.9–5.0 s	>5.0 s

Initial analysis

This article was published in 'Physical Education and the Study of Sport' 4th edn, Davis, B. et al., p. 125, Copyright Elsevier (2000).

Vertical jump (Power)

Test result 1:

Gender	Excellent	Above average	Average	Below average	Poor
Boys	>65 cm	50–65 cm	40–49 cm	30–39 cm	<30 cm
Girls	>58 cm	47–58 cm	36–46 cm	26–35 cm	<26 cm

Initial analysis

This article was published in 'Physical Education and the Study of Sport' 4th edn, Davis, B. et al., p. 123, Copyright Elsevier (2000).

Standing broad jump (Power)

Test result 1:

Gender	Excellent	Above average	Average	Below average	Poor
Boys	>2.26 m	2.11–2.26 m	1.98–2.10 m	1.85–1.97 m	<1.85 m
Girls	>1.85 m	1.73–1.84 m	1.60–1.72 m	1.50–1.59 m	<1.50 m

Initial analysis

Hede, C. et al. (2011) 'PE Senior Physical Education for Queensland' in Brian Mackenzie (n.d.) BrianMac Sports Coach [Online].

Wall sit (Muscular endurance)

Test result 1:

Gender	Excellent	Above average	Average	Below average	Poor
Male	>100 s	75–100 s	50–75 s	25–49 s	<25 s
Female	>60 s	45–60 s	35–44 s	20–34 s	<20 s

Initial analysis

Note: These are norms for adults as no students norms available.

Topend Sports (n.d.) 'Single-Leg Wall Sit Test' in Topend Sports [Online].

Alternate hand wall throw (Coordination) catches in 30 seconds

Test result 1:

Gender	Excellent	Above average	Average	Below average	Poor
Boys	>35	30–35	25–29	20–24	<20
Girls	>35	30–35	25–29	20–24	<20

Initial analysis

Beashal, P. and Taylor, J. (1997) 'The World of Sport Examined' in Brian Mackenzie (n.d.) BrianMac Sports Coach [Online].

Stand stork test (Balance)

Test result 1:

Gender	Excellent	Above average	Average	Below average	Poor
Boys	>50 s	41–50 s	31–40 s	20–30 s	<20 s
Girls	>30 s	23–30 s	16–22 s	10–15 s	<10 s

Self analysis

Johnson, B.L. and Nelson, J.K. (1979) 'Practical Measurements for Evaluation in Physical Education' in Brian Mackenzie (n.d.) BrianMac Sports Coach [Online].

Ruler drop (Reaction time)

Test result 1:

Gender	Excellent	Above average	Average	Below average	Poor
Boys	<7.5 cm	7.5–15.9 cm	15.9–20.4 cm	20.4–28 cm	>28 cm
Girls	<7.5 cm	7.5–15.9 cm	15.9–20.4 cm	20.4–28 cm	>28 cm

Self analysis

This article was published in 'Physical Education and the Study of Sport' 4th edn, Davis, B. et al., p. 130, Copyright Elsevier (2000)

3. **Analyse your results (you may do this by answering some of the following questions):**

   a) What are your thoughts and feelings on your results?

   ....

   ....

   ....

   ....

   b) How did they compare to the national norms?

   ....

   ....

   ....

   c) How far away were you from the next category?

   ....

   ....

   ....

d) What impact does each component of fitness tested have on your performance in your sport or activity?

....

....

....

....

Exam-style questions

1. Describe in detail the procedures for the multi-stage fitness test. (2)

....

....

....

2. Give the definition of *power*. (1)

....

3. Which fitness test could you use to measure power? (1)

....

4. To be useful, results from fitness tests must be both reliable and valid. Discuss what is meant by *reliability* and *validity*. (2)

....

....

5. Identify *two* main components of fitness for a prop in rugby and explain how they would use these to be effective within a game. (3)

....

....

....

....

revisit ◀ reflect ▶ revise!

Look at your class notes on Fitness and Body Systems from your theory work.

- **Revisit** the work completed so far in your personal exercise programme.
- Use Figure 3.3 to **reflect** on your 'initial analysis' where you have compared data against national norms.
- **Revise** any key words and look over the health, fitness and wellbeing topic area in your own notes to help you produce a detailed analysis.

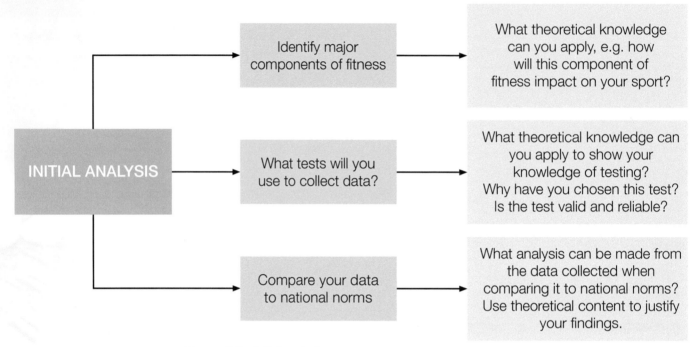

Figure 3.3 Initial analysis

Now that you've had a go, assess your work against the **criteria** and consider the following:

- Based on the content of your work, what level would you place your work at?
- Look back over your work. What do you need to get to the next level?

Remember you're trying to achieve the top level.

WHAT'S MY LEVEL?

Edexcel

Edexcel: level descriptors for initial analysis

Level 1	Level 2	Level 3	Level 4	Level 5
Limited or little interpretation of fitness test results using some data.	Some attempt at interpretation and analysis of fitness test results using some data, but with errors that may impact analysis.	Good interpretation and analysis of fitness test results using appropriate data, with some errors that have insignificant impact on the analysis.	Very good interpretation and analysis of fitness test results using appropriate data, with one or two minor errors not significantly affecting the analysis.	Excellent and thorough interpretation and analysis of fitness test results using appropriate data.

Stretch and challenge: You should be aiming for Level 5!

Hints and tips

- Identify the major components of fitness used for your chosen sport and which ones are specific to your event or playing position.

- Carry out a range of tests. Make sure you know the protocols for the tests you are thinking of carrying out.

- Compare your test scores to the national norms (use the example and tables provided to help you set up and present your analysis).

Links to key areas

Below are recommended links to **Components 1** and **2**. Look over your class notes and apply to your PEP.

Component 1: Fitness and Body Systems

 Topic 3: Physical training (3.1, 3.2, 3.3, 3.5 & 3.6)

Component 2: Health and Performance

 Topic 1: Health, fitness and wellbeing (1.1)

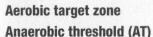 KEY WORDS

Aerobic target zone
Anaerobic threshold (AT)
Anaerobic target zone
Blood pressure (BP)
Cardiovascular system
Components of fitness
Diastolic blood pressure
Duration
Failure
Fartlek training
Field tests
FITT

Frequency
Heart rate (HR)
Intensity
Laboratory tests
Lactic acid system
Maximal force
Muscle endurance
National norms
Normative data
Physical Activity
    Readiness
    Questionnaire (PARQ)
Plyometric

Power
Principles of training
Proprioceptive
    neuromuscular
    facilitation (PNF)
Reliability
Shuttles
Systolic blood pressure
Test protocols
Training zones
Triceps
Validity

Recommendations for improvement – target setting

From the data collected in Chapter 3, you will know what your strengths and weaknesses are in your chosen activity. You can now decide on target areas that will bring about improvements in your performance in this activity or sport.

This chapter will provide an example based on a 400 m sprinter who wishes to bring about improvements within their event.

By the end of this chapter you will:

- Decide upon the component of fitness you will work on through your personal exercise programme.
- Set SMART targets for these improvements.

What to do and why

Before you can plan your personal exercise programme you will need to decide upon a **specific** component of fitness that you will focus on during the six- to eight-week plan. To help with your planning you should then identify target(s) that focus on performance that are **SMART**:

SMART targets are *Specific, Measurable, Achievable, Realistic and Time-bound;* they will give your goals **clarity** and **direction**.

How to do it

To set targets that are specific to helping you bring about improvements in your performance within your chosen activity follow the simple step-by-step instructions:

- Identify SMART target(s) that relate to the component of fitness you have identified as a weakness or one that you think you need to develop further (from your initial analysis in Chapter 3).
- Make sure the number of targets you decide to work on is **manageable** (two or three targets) and that they are **specific** to your chosen activity and component of fitness.
- Select your targets and explain how they link to your chosen activity, component of fitness, event and position.

Use SMART to give you clarity and guidance:

Specific	This must link to your activity and component of fitness. Think about the event or position you are involved in.
Measurable	How will you measure your progress as you work towards your target?
Achievable	Something that is possible for you to do.
Realistic	Are the targets you are setting achievable?
Time-bound	Is the time set for these targets suitable for you achieving your **goals**?

Using your targets, describe recommendations to develop fitness to bring about improvements in performance.

Agreeing a component of fitness goal and setting targets

It is important that the component of fitness that you are going to focus on and the SMART targets are agreed with your coach or teacher at the beginning of your programme; these targets can then be reviewed and monitored throughout the duration of your plan. This will allow you to keep check on progress being made.

Figure 4.1 (on p. 42) and the notes below can be used to guide discussions before, and during, the plan. These will help you collect evidence on recommendations to bring about improvements in performance in your chosen activity.

You may want to use two copies of Figure 4.1 for this profiling exercise:

- one for you as the performer
- one for your teacher or coach.

If you and your coach or teacher complete the pre-meeting sections before the meeting, this will help with the discussions.

Coach/teacher pre-meeting notes
- Reflect on the performer's ability for each component on the radar graph and identify where you would place them. Give the student a mark out of ten for each component of fitness, with 10 been the highest score.
- In the pre-meeting notes section, highlight any points of discussion you would like to talk about with the performer.

Player pre-meeting notes
- Reflect on yourself as a performer and identify where you would place yourself for each component on the radar graph. Give yourself a mark out of ten for each component of fitness, with 10 been the highest score.
- In the pre-meeting notes section, highlight any points of discussion you would like to talk about with your coach/teacher.

Coach/teacher feedback
Make notes on the coach/teacher feedback and record any recommendations suggested.

Player feedback
This section is where you can make notes on your thoughts and reflections based on your coach/teacher feedback and any recommendations suggested.

Meet with your coach or teacher to discuss your goals and how to achieve them

Coach/teacher pre-meeting notes:

....
....
....
....

Player pre-meeting notes:

....
....
....
....

Coach/teacher feedback:

....
....
....
....
....

Player feedback:

....
....
....
....

Recommendations for improvements:

....
....
....
....

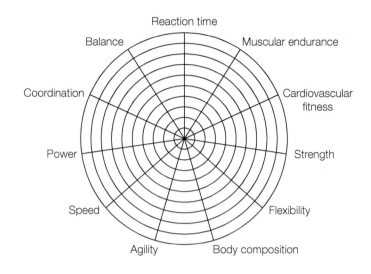

Coach/teacher radar graph

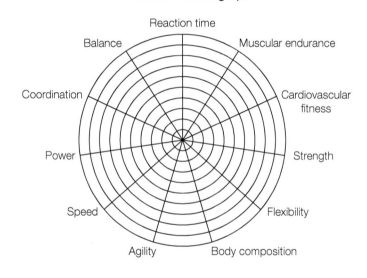

Performer's radar graph

Figure 4.1 Profiling – Coach/teacher and performer review

Recommendations for improvements

Decide upon the component of fitness you want to improve and the target(s) that you are going to use to help you achieve your goal. Discuss a range of recommendations to develop fitness and performance.
These recommendations could be:

- Specific method of training to be used
- Application of **overload** (frequency, intensity and duration)
- Monitoring and adjusting the training plan
- Testing – using data to monitor progress.

Example

Here is an example for a 400 m runner.

Recommendations to bring about improvements in the 400 m

I am a 400 m runner with a PB of 53.06 seconds. My goal is sub 52 seconds so my main goal is to improve my speed. From my test scores in the 30 m sprint test I scored 4 seconds which placed me 'above average' against normative data. My target is to reduce my time by 0.5 seconds, which would then put me into 'excellent' at 4.2 seconds for 30 m when compared to normative data.

As a 400 m sprinter, by improving my speed over the first 50 m of the race, it will allow me to get up to race pace and be in a good place in terms of the stagger coming out of the first bend. By being in a good place at this stage of the race, it will help with motivation and will allow me to settle and relax into my stride in the back straight when I reach the 100 m mark.

Coach/teacher pre-meeting notes:
Three areas to develop:
- *reaction time out of the blocks*
- *speed over the first 50 m*
- *muscular endurance for the later stages of the race.*

Player pre-meeting notes:
I would like to improve my PB and to do this I need to develop my speed at the beginning of race so I can control the race and relax into my technique.

Coach/teacher feedback:
I agree that we should work towards improving your PB and think we should prioritise developing your speed over the first 50 m of a race.

Player feedback:
Both my coach and I identified speed, reaction time and muscular endurance as areas for development. I trust the recommendations of my coach and we will focus on speed.

Recommendations for improvements:
My coach and I have agreed that of the three areas I need to work on, improving my speed over for the first 50 m is the fitness component I need to develop in my PEP.

We will meet again in two weeks' time to discuss progress.

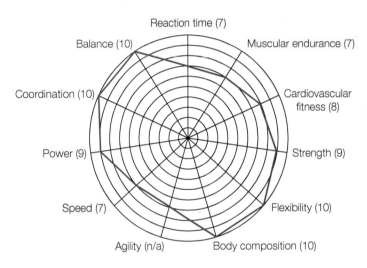

Coach/teacher radar graph

Reaction time (7)
Balance (10)
Muscular endurance (7)
Coordination (10)
Cardiovascular fitness (8)
Power (9)
Strength (9)
Speed (7)
Flexibility (10)
Agility (n/a)
Body composition (10)

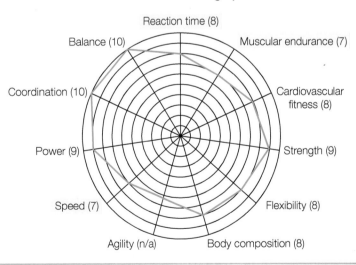

Performer's radar graph

Reaction time (8)
Balance (10)
Muscular endurance (7)
Coordination (10)
Cardiovascular fitness (8)
Power (9)
Strength (9)
Speed (7)
Flexibility (8)
Agility (n/a)
Body composition (8)

Table 4.1   A SMART target for a 400 m sprinter

SMART target	Description of a SMART target
S Specific	My goal is to improve my speed, which is the time taken to get from A to B. The 400 m is about getting from start to finish as fast as possible. My aim is to reduce my time by 0.5 seconds (2.7 sec to 2.2 sec) which would then put me into 'excellent' at 2.2 seconds for 30 m when compared to normative data.
M Measurable	I will use the 30 m sprint test to measure my progress. This test is a **valid** and **reliable** test as it measures speed over a distance. I will complete this test again after four weeks and then again after eight weeks. The reason I will test after four weeks is to see if my PEP is working and to make any adjustment to my programme if I need to.
A Achievable	This target has been agreed as achievable with my county athletics coach, who will also help me to plan my eight-week training plan. This will focus mainly on speed and muscular endurance.
R Realistic	This target is aspirational but realistic in the time we have. We will monitor progress made during the training plan and through races over the next eight weeks. As I see the improvement, this will **motivate** me to work more towards my target. My 400 m PB is 53.06 seconds and my goal is below 52 seconds.
T Time-bound	My personalised exercise programme is set for a minimum of eight weeks. My coach and I believe the target is achievable over this time, and we will prepare the training to meet the deadline. We will monitor the progress through training and testing.

PB stands for 'personal best'.

Athlete competing in a 400 m event

Have a go!

Introduction

When writing about your recommendations for improvement, you need to think about the following questions:

What's your background?

....

....

....

....

Why have you decided upon this component of fitness?

....

....

....

By improving this component of fitness what impact will it have on your chosen activity?

....

....

....

What will you be hoping to achieve by the end of the programme?

....

....

....

....

Target setting

i) Complete this profiling – coach/teacher and performer review

Coach/teacher pre-meeting notes:

....

....

....

....

Player pre-meeting notes:

....

....

....

....

Coach/teacher feedback:

....

....

....

....

....

Player feedback:

....

....

....

....

Recommendations for improvements:

....

....

....

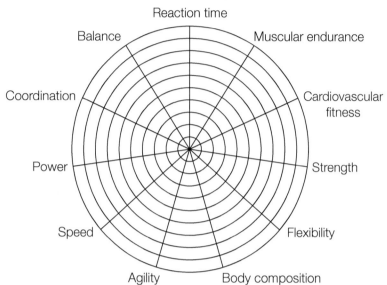

Coach/teacher radar graph

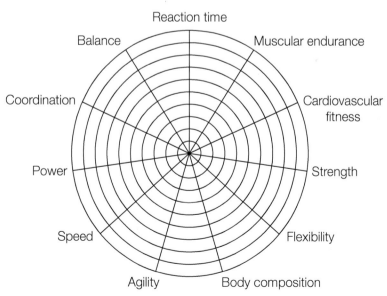

Performer's radar graph

ii) Use Table 4.2 to plan your targets.

Use the example of the 400 m runner to guide you through your planning of SMART targets.

Table 4.2   My SMART target

SMART target	Description of a SMART target
S Specific	
M Measurable	
A Achievable	
R Realistic	
T Time-bound	

Exam-style questions

1. When setting goals to improve performance in physical activity, applying SMART targets is a key factor for success. Explain what SMART stands for. (1)

2. Explain why targets need to be measurable. (1)

3. Explain how a 400m runner could use SMART targets in training for their event. (6)

4. Give an example of a measurable target that could be set for a sprinter. (1)

5. State why it is good practice to agree your target with a coach or teacher. (1)

revisit ◀ reflect ▶ revise!

This is an opportunity for you to apply theoretical content to your PEP.
- **Revisit** the work completed so far in your PEP.
- i) Using Figure 4.2 **reflect** on your 'Recommendations for improvements' section where you have set targets. Check you have included all of these aspects.
  ii) **Reflect** on your targets. Are they SMART? See the checklist in Table 4.3.
- **Revise** any key words and look over Component 2: Health and Performance 'Topic 1: Health, fitness and wellbeing' and 'Topic 2: Sports psychology' to provide detailed recommendations. Then apply your knowledge and understanding to your 'Recommendations for improvement' section.

Detailed recommendations

- Specific
- Measurable
- Achievable
- Realistic
- Time-bound
- Valid test
- Reliable test

- Method of training
- Principle of training
- Motivation
- Monitoring
- Use of data

Figure 4.2 Do your 'Recommendations for improvements' reflect these elements?

Table 4.3 Checklist for a SMART target

Specific	You are aware of the specific training requirements linked to your component of fitness.
Measurable	The test is valid and reliable and will help monitor progress.
Achievable	Something that is possible for you to do.
Realistic	You will have a high chance of achieving improvements.
Time-bound	The set time will allow you to see improvements.

Now that you've had a go, assess your work against the criteria and consider the following:

- Based on the content of your work, what level would you place your work in?
- Look back over your work. What do you need to get to the next level?

Remember you're trying to achieve the top level.

WHAT'S MY LEVEL?

Edexcel: level descriptors for initial evaluation

Edexcel

Level 1	Level 2	Level 3	Level 4	Level 5
Limited evaluation (mainly descriptive) resulting in inappropriate selection of training method(s) and little application of SMART targets and principles of training to meet performance goal(s).	Some attempts at evaluation, with weak justification for training method(s) chosen, and attempts at applying SMART targets and principles of training to meet performance goal(s), with errors of judgement affecting the quality of the evaluation.	Good evaluation with appropriate training method(s) selected and explained, and application of SMART targets and principles of training to meet performance goal(s), with some errors of judgement that have insignificant impact on the evaluation.	Evaluation with appropriate training method(s) selected and explained, and application of SMART targets and principles of training to meet performance goal(s), with few errors of judgement not significantly affecting the evaluation.	Evaluation with appropriate training method(s) selected and justified, and application of SMART targets and principles of training to meet performance goal(s).

This chapter focuses on the identification of a component of fitness and the application of SMART targets to meet performance goals elements of the initial evaluation level descriptors.

Hints and tips

- State the component of fitness you are going to address in your PEP.

- Present your SMART targets clearly.

- Try to complete two or three 'profiling – coach/teacher and performer reviews' throughout your PEP. They will add supporting evidence and help you to provide detailed recommendations to improve.

KEY WORDS

Goals
Motivation
Overload
Reliable
SMART target
Valid

Links to key areas

Below are recommended links to **Components 1** and **2**. Look over your class notes and apply to your PEP.

Component 1: Fitness and Body Systems

 Topic 3: Physical training (3.2, 3.3, 3.4 & 3.6)

 Topic 4: Use of data (4.1)

Component 2: Health and Performance

 Topic 2: Sports psychology (2.2, 2.3 & 2.4)

Planning and monitoring your PEP

5

You are now ready to plan your personal exercise programme (PEP) based on the component of fitness you have chosen to improve. This chapter will help you understand how to do this. It will give you ideas on how to carry out your PEP and monitor your progress so you can adapt and change the training programme as you go along to suit your needs. This chapter also provides an example training plan for a rugby player who wishes to improve key targets in their sport. This example will give you some ideas on how to plan and complete your own PEP.

By the end of this chapter you will:

- Design and follow a personalised exercise programme with the aim of achieving the SMART targets associated with your chosen component of fitness.
- Collect data to monitor your performance during this task to see if your training programme has helped you improve your personal exercise performance and achieve your target or targets.
- Adapt and change your training programme if required.

What to do and why

Here are the stages of planning and monitoring your PEP, as summarised in Figure 5.1 (on p. 52).

- Complete a Physical Activity Readiness Questionnaire or **PARQ** to determine the safety or possible risk of you completing your PEP based on your health history.
- Based on one method of training design a **training plan** that you think will help you to improve your chosen component of fitness.
- Follow your training plan for six to eight weeks; your teacher will tell you how long for.
- Plan to have at least two or three training sessions every week for the duration of your PEP.
- During your training programme you need to **record data** on a training record form (see Appendix 5, p. 112) for each session.
- On several occasions during your PEP, at least every two/three weeks, carry out fitness testing to **monitor** and **measure** any changes in your fitness and **performance data**.
- Following the principles of training, **adapt and change** your training programme where necessary.
- If you make changes to your training programme, **highlight** and **explain** any **adaptations** in a personal log or diary.

PARQ

↓

Training plan

↓

Training

↓

Recording data

↓

Monitoring and measuring

↓

Adapting and changing

↓

Highlighting and explaining

Figure 5.1 Planning and monitoring your PEP

Monitoring and recording your progress during this activity will help you see if your training plan is enabling you to improve the component of fitness you have identified. **Adapting** your training programme as you go along will show that you are aware of the effects of your sessions and how they can be improved to make sure you achieve your key target.

How to do it

Step-by-step instructions:

- Fill in your PARQ
- Plan your personal exercise programme (PEP) based on one method of training and one component of fitness.
- When you are writing your training plan make sure you use appropriate principles of training:
  - ○ specific to targets
  - ○ **progressive overload: FITT (frequency, intensity**, time, type)
- Decide on how you are going to record your data. Use tables, training record forms, a logbook or diary, or a combination of these.
- Set the start date for your training programme.
- Make sure you have all the facilities and equipment you need to carry out your chosen training programme and to monitor your performance.
- Ask other students to help you measure and record your performance if required.

You need to test the effects of your training programme on your fitness and performance target at several stages:

1. at the start
2. every two or three weeks, or at the mid-point
3. at the end.

Rugby players involved in a ruck

Have you got everything you need organised and ready?

During the period of the training sessions, adapt and change your training programme depending on your test results and progress made throughout your plan.

Personal log or diary

Here are some areas you need to write about in your personal log or diary:

- **application** of theory, effects of exercise, etc.
- factors that may have impacted on your session
- what you think about your **levels of fitness**
- how you coped with the session
- **adapting** the plan for your next session.

Example

Here is an example PEP that shows a possible approach to producing a personal exercise plan:

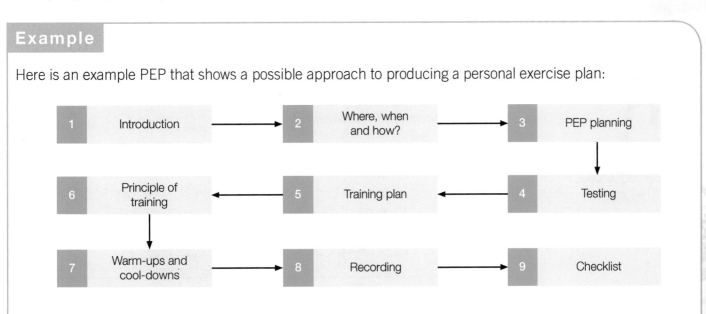

Step 1: Introduction

I have chosen rugby as the focus for my PEP as it is my favourite sport and I play for the school under-16 team on Wednesdays and for my local rugby club on Sundays.

As a second row rugby player my key movement component is lineout jumping and my most important physical abilities are speed, strength and reactive strength. Last season I was consistently winning six to eight balls in the lineout over the course of a match. However, this season I believe that I am not winning enough balls at lineouts, particularly in the second half of a game as my average is down to four to six balls won. I want to increase this average above last season's and to do that I feel that I need to be able to jump higher and sustain this over time, so I can increase the lineouts I win over the duration of a match. The component of fitness I will focus on will be power.

Objective:

- To jump consistently higher in lineouts in order to increase the average number of balls I win to nine over the duration of a competitive rugby match.

Pre-training test:

- Vertical jump test

Aim:

To increase my success rates in lineouts during a match, I need to improve the power of my muscles, in particular my leg muscles, so I am able to increase the height of my jump to catch or intercept the ball. Over the eight weeks of my training plan I aim to increase my vertical jump height by 6 cm.

Step 2: Where, when and how?

- I shall decide on which date I am going to start my PEP.
- All my training sessions will take place in the sports hall.
- Each training session will last one hour allowing 20 minutes for warm-up and cool-down.
- I plan to have two sessions every week for eight weeks.
- I will need a variety of equipment.
- I shall also need other students to assist me with the testing.

Step 3: PEP planning

To help produce my PEP, I have used SMART targets to make sure it is effective in achieving my aim:

S Specific	My goal is to improve my power. My target is to increase my vertical jump height by 6 cm by the end of my PEP. I also want to increase the number of line-outs I win during competitive matches to nine.
M Measurable	I will measure my target through the vertical jump test and by recording line-out success in future rugby matches.

Reminder: Look back to Table 3.2, p.23, for more information on these tests.

See p.31 for the national norm and p.34 for the vertical jump test data.

Reminder: See Chapter 4 for more on SMART targets.

A Achievable	My aim was set to a level I could achieve over the eight-week period of the PEP.
R Realistic	The targets I have set are achievable if I make the maximum effort during training sessions.
T Time-bound	My PEP is planned for eight weeks with two training sessions every week.

As well as considering SMART targets, I have also taken into account the methods of training and **FITT** (frequency, intensity, time and type) principles of training when planning and completing my PEP (see Table 5.1).

Table 5.1 FITT principles of training

Frequency	I shall carry out my training sessions twice each week during my PE lessons.
Intensity	I will begin the training sessions at a suitable level for my fitness and will adjust over the duration of my training programme based on my tests and progress over the eight weeks.
Time	As rugby matches consist of 40-minute halves, I will plan sessions of this length, excluding my warm-ups and cool-downs.
Type	With my focus fitness component of improving my leg power, I have chosen to follow circuit training including single and double leg box jumps.

When considering methods of training, I decided that interval training, in the form of a circuit, was the most suitable method to achieve my targets. These high intensity **anaerobic** exercises mimic the stop–start nature of a rugby match.

Step 4: Testing

To measure my jump height, I am going to use the vertical jump test.

Table 5.2 Choosing tests for my chosen fitness component

Fitness component	Fitness test	Why test chosen
Power	Vertical jump	Tests how high I can jump, is easily measured and relates to my rugby key target. Determines if training will make a difference in my overall leg power and rugby-specific target. Can indicate risk of injury or loss of performance due to fatigue.

Reminder: Look back to Chapter 3 for more information on fitness tests.

Vertical jump:

- Before this test, I will perform a short warm-up, including jogging and stretching.
- I will stand beside a wall with a measuring board and with a piece of chalk in the hand nearest the wall.

- To measure my standing reach, I will touch the wall as high as I can with my hand and use the chalk to leave a mark on the wall.
- Then I will jump as high as I can from a flat-footed position and touch the highest point on the wall I can reach.
- I will repeat three times.
- The distance between the first mark on the wall (standing reach) and the highest point on the wall (point of highest jump) is my standing vertical jump height.
- I will write this down in my recording table.

Advantages of performing the vertical jump test:

- The test is quick and easy to perform.
- It is inexpensive to do as little equipment is required.
- It is a good way to assess anaerobic leg power and jumping ability.
- The test is easily repeatable.
- There are standard norms to measure against.

Disadvantages of performing the vertical jump test:

- During the vertical jump test, technique may play a bigger part than leg power.
- Using chalk to record a jump may allow errors when recording accurate scores.

I will carry out my pre-test vertical jump test before my first training session and then re-test every two or three weeks to see if my training is working.

If required, I will change the intensity of the **reps** or timing of my circuit over the duration of the weeks, according to the results of my vertical jump tests.

Step 5: Training plan

Now moving on to my PEP, I need to select a method of training that will increase the chances of achieving my key targets. Therefore, it is important to select a training programme that relates well to my activity and the component of fitness I aim to improve.

Table 5.3   Training method justification table

Fitness component	Possible methods of training	Method chosen	Selection justification
Power	Plyometrics Weight training Isometric stretching Resistance band training	Circuit	I chose to design a circuit as it gives the opportunity to focus on explosive movements and strength that will enable me to use my quad muscles in short powerful bursts; this mimics rugby. I can also include isometric exercises as they can improve the body's ability to apply power from a static position, similar to a lineout.

With the above in mind, I have decided to follow a circuit plan which includes: box jumps; sit-ups; squat jumps; triceps dips; step-ups; forearm plank; single-leg jumps and shuttle runs.

This is the layout of my circuit, which I will put in my Appendix.

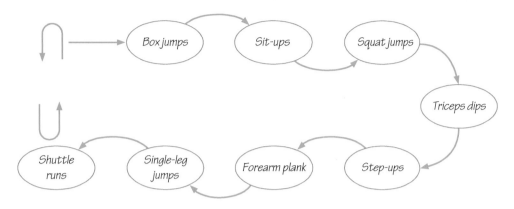

Table 5.4   Explanation of exercise choice

Station number	Exercise (description)	Explanation of exercise choice
1	Box jumps	Plyometric exercise to improve power in the legs
2	Sit-ups	Muscle strengthening and core strength
3	Squat jumps	Plyometric exercise to improve power in the legs
4	Triceps dips	Muscle strengthening
5	Step-ups	Muscle strengthening to help leg power
6	Forearm plank	Isometric exercise for core strength
7	Single-leg jumps	Plyometric exercise to improve power in the legs
8	Shuttle runs	A dynamic exercise that targets the **quadriceps**, hamstrings, gluteus muscles and calves. It also works the hips, obliques, **abdominal muscles** and the lower back. Shuttle runs will also help develop power.

Description of the exercises follows. This will be in my Appendix:

1. **Box jumps:** This exercise involves jumping on and off a box taking off with both feet. This exercise will improve both my strength and speed therefore increasing my power. Box jumps can put a strain on my joints, so I have to be careful to use a good technique to avoid injury. Bending my knees when landing on the box and floor is a good example of this.
2. **Sit-ups:** For this exercise I will lie flat on my back, lift my torso to a sitting position, and then lie flat again without changing the position of my legs and with my knees bent throughout. It is an abdominal endurance training exercise to strengthen and tone the abdominal muscles.
3. **Squat jumps:** This exercise strengthens my **gluteus maximus** and quadriceps; this will help me to develop a more powerful jump.
4. **Triceps dips:** Using a bench for support, with my body in a straight position facing upwards, I shall dip my shoulders which will strengthen my triceps and deltoids. This will be useful when competing for the ball in a rugby lineout.
5. **Step-ups:** Stepping onto and off a bench, this exercise will help develop my quadriceps and my muscular endurance, which will help me to maintain my jump power throughout a game of rugby. Note, I shall lead with different legs during consecutive circuits.
6. **Forearm plank:** In this isometric exercise, I need to keep my spine in a straight line and tighten my abdominal muscles (abs) as much as I can. This a core body exercise that strengthens not only my abdominal and lower back muscles, but also my shoulders and upper back. This strength will come in useful when competing against an opponent in the lineout.

7. **Single-leg jumps:** This exercise involves jumping onto a low box taking off from one leg only. This will use my quadriceps and therefore increase strength and speed (power).

8. **Shuttle runs:** This exercise involves me running back and forth between two points. This will help me to develop my acceleration, speed and my anaerobic fitness. This should help me maintain a high skill level throughout a game of rugby.

To complete my circuits I will need the following equipment:

- Bench
- Stopwatch/timer
- Box
- Gym mat
- Bollards
- Chalk
- Wall with measure board
- Bleep test CD
- CD player.

Note, I shall be monitoring my targets on a weekly basis and may increase or decrease reps and times accordingly as the weeks pass.

Table 5.5   My planned exercise programme

Station	Exercise	Wk 1	Wk 2	Wk 3	Wk 4	Wk 5	Wk 6	Wk 7	Wk 8
		Targets (number or secs)							
1	Box jumps	10	13	16	19	22	25	27	30
2	Sit-ups	10	12	14	16	18	20	22	24
3	Squat jumps	10	12	14	16	18	20	22	24
4	Triceps dips	10	12	14	16	18	20	22	24
5	Step-ups	10	13	16	19	22	25	27	30
6	Forearm plank	20 s	25 s	30 s	35 s	40 s	50 s	60 s	70 s
7	Single-leg jumps	5 per leg	7 per leg	9 per leg	11 per leg	13 per leg	15 per leg	17 per leg	20 per leg
8	Shuttle runs	5	7	9	11	13	15	17	19

Make sure the activities you choose improve your performance and are based on training principles

Step 6: Principles of training

All training programmes aim to improve performance so my exercise sessions are based on these training principles.

Table 5.6   Meeting the principles of training

Principle of training	How my programme meets this principle
Specificity	My training has been designed so it includes elements that are specific to jumping in a lineout during a rugby match.
Progressive overload	I will start with a low number of reps and durations that suit my fitness. As the weeks pass, I will increase the number of reps or seconds taken for each exercise. I have planned to train twice a week, but if my fitness allows I may increase that at some point (or I may increase the length of each training session).
Type	In order to keep my sessions interesting, I will make sure that during my training sessions I will adjust reps, duration and recovery times. Also, if I pick up an injury I will adjust my training accordingly.

Step 7: Warm-ups and cool-downs

Warm-up:

Before every training session I will carry out a warm-up as this will not only increase the blood flow to my muscles it will also stretch my muscles. In addition, a warm-up will increase the temperature of my muscles, **ligaments** and **tendons**; this means I am less likely to injure myself during my training sessions.

Following is a description of the warm-up that I intend to use before each training session. These will include the three phases of a warm-up:

1. Heart/pulse raisers
2. Mobility
3. Skills-based activity.

Table 5.7   Warm-ups

Heart/pulse raisers		
I shall jog for one minute around the sports hall.	I shall continue to jog for a further minute while alternating from high knees, jumping up, running side-to-side and cross-over running.	Finally, I shall continue to jog normally for 10 seconds, and then sprint for five seconds before slowing back to a jog. I will repeat three times.
Mobility: Stretches		
Forward lunges for 30 seconds across the sports hall.	Side lunges: 15 secs for each leg.	Triceps stretches: 15 seconds for each arm.
Arm stretch and pull: 15 seconds for each arm.	Hip rotations: 15 seconds anti-clockwise and 15 seconds clockwise.	Back and leg stretch: 15 seconds for each leg.
Skill-based activity		
10 m shuttle run placing rugby ball down and picking up at mid-point (10 shuttles).	Throwing up a rugby ball and catching at highest point with two hands (10 reps).	20 m zig-zag runs through bollards holding the rugby ball in two hands (10 runs).

Cool-down:

After every training session, I shall cool down as it helps the body to recover after vigorous exercise. It helps to reduce the amount of lactic acid in the muscles, lowers the heart rate towards normal and helps with the removal of carbon dioxide. My cool-down will include these three phases:

1. *Heart rate reducer/pulse reducer*
2. *Mobility*
3. *Refuel.*

Table 5.8   Cool-downs

Heart rate reducers/pulse reducers		
I shall jog normally for 30 seconds and then slow down to a walk for another 30 seconds.	*Then I shall jog on the spot for 30 seconds.*	*Then a brisk walk round the sports hall for four laps.*
Mobility: stretches		
I will stretch each hamstring while sitting on the floor in a hurdling position: two × 20 seconds for each leg.	*Then standing up, I will bring my heels up to my backside to stretch my quads: two × 20 seconds for each leg.*	*To stretch my chest muscles, I shall grasp my hands behind my back and then, keeping upright, lift my arms as high as possible: 30 seconds.*
To stretch my shoulder muscles, I shall cross one arm across my body and stretch it with the other arm. Repeat with the other arm: two × 20 seconds for each arm.	*Then lying on the floor, I shall warm down my lower body by doing scissor kicks: 30 seconds.*	*I shall stretch my back by performing C arches while on my knees: 30 seconds.*
Refuel		
To help me rehydrate, I shall drink a sports drink after I have completed my sessions.	*I shall also eat a high-carbohydrate snack, either a banana or an energy bar.*	

Step 8: Recording

I use this individual training session recording sheet for every session I complete. Here is my one for week 3, session 5; I will include all of them in my Appendix.

Individual sessions record sheet: Date: _____   Week/session no. Week 3, session 5

	Set one		Set two	
Exercises	Target reps or time	Completed	Target reps or time	Completed
Box jumps	16	✓	16	✓
Sit-ups	14	✓	14	✓
Squat jumps	14	✓	14	✓
Triceps dips	14	✓	14	✓
Step-ups	16	✓	16	✓
Forearm plank	30 seconds	✓	30 seconds	✓
Single-leg jumps	9 per leg	✓	9 per leg	✓
Shuttle runs	9	✓	9	✓

Pre-exercise heart rate before warm-up	Working heart rate (b.p.m.)	Immediate post-exercise heart rate (b.p.m.)
71	134	130

	1 min	2 min	3 min	4 min	5 min
Recovery heart rate at the following intervals (b.p.m.)	125	119	105	87	76

Description of training session appropriate to the method of training, e.g. map of continuous training course, plan of circuit training session.

Week 3 Session 5

Warm-up and cool-down: I continued to follow my warm-up and cool-down activities as detailed in my plan (see below for adaptations to numbers to match my increased fitness levels).

Circuit plan x 2 sets

Station	Exercise	Reps
1	Box jumps	18
2	Sit-ups	18
3	Squat jumps	16
4	Triceps dips	18
5	Step-ups	18
6	Forearm plank	32 seconds
7	Single-leg jumps	10 per leg
8	Shuttle runs	11

Any adaptions or changes I have made to this training session and why.

During my warm-up I increased the number of rugby ball shuttles and zig-zag runs from 9 to 11 as I'm getting fitter. I felt this got me fully warmed up and prepared for my circuit training.

In this session I used progressive overload by increasing the number of reps at each station and the number of shuttles during both my circuits. This provided me with a challenge and helped to build both my power and cardiovascular fitness at a faster rate.

Results table:

This is the table I used to record results and to check my progress during my PEP.

Tests/exercise	Pre test	Wk 1		Wk 2		Wk 3		Wk 4		Mid test	Wk 5		Wk 6		Wk 7		Wk 8		Post test
Sessions		1	2	3	4	5	6	7	8		9	10	11	12	13	14	15	16	
Vertical jump	60 cm									64 cm									67 cm
Box jumps		10	10	13	13	18	16	20	20		22	22	25	25	28	28	30	30	
Sit-ups		10	10	12	12	18	16	18	16		20	20	22	22	24	24	26	26	
Squat jumps		10	10	12	12	16	14	18	18		20	20	22	22	24	24	26	26	
Triceps dips		10	10	12	12	18	16	18	18		20	20	20	20	22	22	24	24	
Step-ups		10	10	13	13	18	18	20	20		22	22	25	25	28	28	30	30	
Forearm plank (secs)		20	20	25	25	32	32	35	35		40	40	50	50	60	60	70	70	
Single-leg jumps		5	5	7		10	10	12	12		14	14	16	16	18	18	20	20	
Shuttle runs		5	5	7		11	11	11	11		13	13	15	15	18	18	20	20	

Step 9: Checklist

Here is my progress check table that helped me make sure I completed all the required steps for my PEP as I carried it out.

	Wk 1		Wk 2		Wk 3		Wk 4		Wk 5		Wk 6		Wk 7		Wk 8	
Sessions	1	2	3	4	5	6	7	8	9	10	11	12	13	14	15	16
Circuit completed	✓	✓	✓	✓	✓	✓	✓	✓	✓	✓	✓	✓	✓	✓	✓	✓
Results recorded	✓	✓	✓	✓	✓	✓	✓	✓	✓	✓	✓	✓	✓	✓	✓	✓
Logbook/diary / training record form done	✓	✓	✓	✓	✓	✓	✓	✓	✓	✓	✓	✓	✓	✓	✓	✓
Performance factor measured	✓	✗	✗	✗	✗	✗	✗	✓	✗	✗	✗	✗	✗	✗	✗	✓
Match played	✗	✗	✗	✓	✗	✗	✗	✓	✗	✓	✗	✗	✗	✓	✗	✓

Be sure to methodically record your progress

Have a go!

Now write some notes to help you plan what to include in your PEP. You could include some of the ideas below, or use the rugby example to help you – but remember you need to produce your own PEP, tailored to your strengths, weaknesses and goals.

Step 1: Introduction

Plan a short introduction, including your:

- background and how you got interested in your sport

....

....

....

- objectives

....

....

....

- pre-training tests

....

....

....

- aims

....

....

....

Step 2: Where, when and how?

- State when you are going to carry out your training, e.g. start and finish dates.

....

- Select when you will carry out your training, e.g. during PE lessons.

....

● Decide where will you do it, e.g. sports hall, track, field.

....

● Choose how long each training session will last, e.g. warm-up, session and cool-down.

....

● Decide on the number of training sessions per week.

....

● Think about the equipment available to you, e.g. benches, mats, stopwatches.

....

● Describe what help, if any, you will need, e.g. other students to help with recording and measuring.

....

Step 3: PEP planning

i) Note down the SMART targets you planned in Chapter 4.

SMART target	Description of a SMART target
S Specific	
M Measurable	
A Achievable	
R Realistic	
T Time-bound	

ii) Note down some ideas for your FITT principles of training table.

Frequency	
Intensity	
Time	
Type	

Step 4: Testing

- Write the types of test and fitness components in the table.

Fitness component	Fitness test	Why test was chosen

- Explain how you are going to perform these tests.

....

....

- Identify the advantages and disadvantages of your tests.

....

....

....

....

- Explain when you intend to carry out your testing e.g. pre, mid and post.

....

Step 5: Training plan

● Use the table to help you choose your method of training.

Fitness component	Possible methods of training	Method chosen	Selection justification

● Outline the particular exercises you are going to use.

....

....

● Produce information or a sketch/drawing/plan of your training sessions.

Station number	Exercise (description)	Explanation of exercise choice
1		
2		
3		
4		
5		
6		
7		
8		

● Describe each exercise and explain why you are including it in your plan.

....

....

....

....

....

....

....

....

....

....

....

....

....

● List the equipment you are intending to use e.g. benches, mats, stopwatches etc.

....

....

....

....

- Produce your planned training programme table to show your targets for each training session.

Station	Exercises	Wk 1	Wk 2	Wk 3	Wk 4	Wk 5	Wk 6	Wk 7	Wk 8
		Targets (number or secs)							
1									
2									
3									
4									
5									
6									
7									
8									

Step 6: Principles of training

Complete the principles of training table and explain how your programme meets each principle (more rows can be added if required).

Principle of training	How my programme meets this principle

Step 7: Warm-ups and cool-downs

- Plan the warm-ups for your training sessions and explain why you have selected them.

....

....

....

....

....

....

....

....

- Produce a warm-up table to illustrate your plan.

Heart/pulse raisers		
Mobility: stretches		
Skill-based activity		

- Plan your cool-downs, again stating why you have chosen them.

....

....

....

....

....

Heart rate reducers/pulse reducers		

Mobility: stretches		

Refuel	

Step 8: Recording

Create a training record form for every session you intend to do. A training record form, like the example here, must be completed (and submitted as evidence) for every training session you carry out. You can find a copy of Edexcel's full PEP training record form in Appendix 5 (p. 112).

Individual sessions record sheet:	Date: _____		Week/session number: _____	
	Circuit one		**Circuit two**	
Exercises	Target reps or time	Completed	Target reps or time	Completed

Pre-exercise heart rate before warm-up	Working heart rate (b.p.m.)	Immediate post-exercise heart rate (b.p.m.)

	1 min	2 min	3 min	4 min	5 min
Recovery heart rate at the following intervals (b.p.m.)					

Description of training session appropriate to the method of training, e.g. map of continuous training course, plan of circuit training session.

Any adaptions or changes I have made to this training session and why.

Produce a table like this one to record pre- and post-testing results and to monitor your progress as you complete your PEP.

Tests/exercise	Pre test	Wk 1		Wk 2		Wk 3		Wk 4		Mid test	Wk 5		Wk 6		Wk 7		Wk 8		Post test
Sessions		1	2	3	4	5	6	7	8		9	10	11	12	13	14	15	16	

Step 9: Checklists

● Produce a progress check table in order to monitor and track your progress and make sure you are up to date with your recording of results.

Sessions	Wk 1		Wk 2		Wk 3		Wk 4		Wk 5		Wk 6		Wk 7		Wk 8	
	1	2	3	4	5	6	7	8	9	10	11	12	13	14	15	16
Circuit completed																
Results recorded																
Logbook/diary/training record form done																
Performance factor measured																
Match played																

Now that you have planned your PEP you now need to complete it. Here is a checklist to help you. Start your six- to eight-week programme on your planned start date and time.

> Tick each part when you have completed it.

☐ Make sure you keep a record in your progress table, training record form, logbook or diary for all sessions that you complete.

☐ Have a review discussion after each training session. Talk about how it went, what you think about your level of fitness and performance, and how easy or difficult you found the session.

☐ Your records should describe how you feel and how closely training sessions match your plans, e.g. make comments on your post-exercise heart rate to help you monitor how hard you worked in the session.

☐ Follow your training programme for two or three weeks.

☐ At this point, collect performance data for your key target to see if you are making progress towards improving it.

☐ Carry out mid-point testing.

☐ If needed, make changes to your plan if you think this would help to improve the chances of achieving your SMART target(s).

☐ Continue with your updated plan for another two or three weeks.

☐ Evaluate and test again.

☐ Make further changes if required.

☐ Complete your updated training plan.

Exam-style questions

1. Discuss why it is important that a sportsperson regularly monitors their performance. (6)

See Appendix 3, p.108 for the answers.

2. A student would like to increase their performance level and fitness in their hockey game. Their coach suggests circuit training as a useful method to use. Give two advantages of using circuit training to increase fitness and performance levels. (2)

3. Physical fitness testing is an important part of a training programme. Give four reasons why this is the case. (4)

....

....

....

....

....

....

....

....

....

....

revisit ◄ reflect ► revise!

- **Revisit** the work completed so far in this chapter.
- **Reflect** on and make sure you have shown understanding of each of these terms:
  - Specificity
  - Overload
  - Methods of training
  - Training zones
  - Reps and sets.
- **Revise** any key words. Work through the health and performance component to provide detailed information.

Now that you've had a go, assess your work against the criteria and consider the following:

- Based on the content of your work, what level would you place your work at?
- Look back over your work. What do you need to get to the next level?

Remember you're trying to achieve the top level.

WHAT'S MY LEVEL?

Edexcel: level descriptors for initial evaluation

Edexcel

Level 1	Level 2	Level 3	Level 4	Level 5
Limited evaluation (mainly descriptive) resulting in inappropriate selection of training method(s) and little application of SMART targets and principles of training to meet performance goal(s).	Some attempts at evaluation, with weak justification for training method(s) chosen, and attempts at applying SMART targets and principles of training to meet performance goal(s), with errors of judgement affecting the quality of the evaluation.	Good evaluation with appropriate training method(s) selected and explained, and application of SMART targets and principles of training to meet performance goal(s), with some errors of judgement that have insignificant impact on the evaluation.	Evaluation with appropriate training method(s) selected and explained, and application of SMART targets and principles of training to meet performance goal(s), with few errors of judgement not significantly affecting the evaluation.	Evaluation with appropriate training method(s) selected and justified, and application of SMART targets and principles of training to meet performance goal(s).

Links to key areas

Below are recommended links to **Components 1** and **2**. Look over your class notes and apply to your PEP.

Component 1: Fitness and Body Systems

 Topic 3: Physical training (3.2, 3.3 & 3.6)

Component 2: Health and Performance

 Topic 1: Health, fitness and wellbeing (1.1)

 Topic 2: Sports psychology (2.2, 2.3 & 2.4)

KEY WORDS

Abdominal muscle	Frequency	Progressive overload
Adaptations	Gluteus maximus	Quadriceps
Aerobic	Intensity	Reps
Anaerobic	Isometric stretching	Specificity
Duration	Ligaments	Tendons
Dynamic stretching	Overload	Triceps
FITT	Plyometrics	Variance

Hints and tips

- Make sure you use a personal training record form for every one of your training sessions.
- Write up your training log or diary as soon as possible after every session
- Have a discussion with your peers teacher after every training session to reflect on how it went.
- Keep referring to your training plan checklist (see p.72) to ensure you have covered all tasks required to complete your PEP.
- Keep checking your lesson notes to link your activity to theory (see the links to key areas).

6 Post-PEP analysis and evaluation of data and programme

Now that you have completed your PEP you need to look at the results of your training and use them to show how effective it was in achieving the desired changes in fitness, and, most importantly, how it impacted on your performance goal.

What to do and why

You need to look at all the results you recorded during your PEP and then assess and draw up your post-test data to see if you achieved your component of fitness target. Then, to help you to measure the overall effectiveness of your PEP, compare your pre-fitness testing and performance data. Finally, you need to **evaluate** how your method of training, SMART goals and principles of training impacted on your performance.

How to do it

In order to evaluate your PEP, you need to follow these steps:

Step 1

- Collect and draw up the post-PEP data you have collected during your training programme from your training record forms/logbooks/diary/tables etc. You need to refer to the fitness testing data that relates to the component of fitness you have been trying to improve.
- Use graphs, charts, tables and diagrams to illustrate your results visually. They should be used to support your analysis and evaluation of your findings.
- Present your results in a clear **logical** way.
- Compare your results with **normative data**.
- Draw up conclusions that are logical and demonstrate **validity**.
- Write a statement summarising your results and whether you succeeded or not in achieving your fitness and performance target.

Step 2

- Compare pre-, mid- and post-PEP fitness and performance data.
- Analyse the data gathered and any changes specific to your focus activity.
- Draw valid and logical conclusions.
- Write a statement about the overall effectiveness of your PEP in improving your sporting performance. You need to refer to evidence which supports your improvements in fitness and performance, or provide reasons why any improvements did not occur.

> Make sure you show a clear **correlation** between your PEP and the impact on your performance.

Step 3

Evaluate the application of the method of training, SMART goals and principles of training in your PEP by writing a statement about each of the following:

  i) Did your method of training cause the changes to your performance you needed in order to improve your fitness?

  ii) Were your SMART targets achieved?

  iii) Have you applied the principles of training appropriately?

> Use the data collected in your activity/sporting performance to feed back into the evaluation of the PEP.

Example

I am a 15-year-old golfer who plays for the junior team at their local golf club.

My main aim this season is to consistently drive the ball off the tee with my driver. As my club head speed is already good, I have decided to concentrate on developing my power. My target is to add another 15 metres to my drives.

My other aim this season is to reduce my golf handicap from 16 to 14. I believe I can achieve this target if I am able to drive the ball further.

From the pre- and post-PEP data I collected during my training sessions, which I recorded in tables and in my logbook, I drew up the results tables which can be found in Appendix 1.

Evaluation:

My main target of improving my driving distance was achieved as my average driving distance improved over the period of my PEP. I also reduced my playing handicap to 15 during the duration of my PEP.

Overall my PEP was successful as my pre- and post-PEP results (Appendix 1) show that, not only did I reduce my handicap, I improved my average driving distance from 230 m to 250 m, improving by 20 m, which was 5 m more than my target. I was very pleased with this, as driving length has been an issue with me in the past. Therefore I was very happy with my programme as I exceeded my SMART target. With improved power, I can now hit the ball further off the tee, which means I can use a shorter club for my next shot.

Test results:

At the start of my PEP I was able to complete my circuit training without too much difficulty, but my grip dynamometer data showed that I was not improving my strength. Based on evaluating each session, I reviewed my SMART targets at the end of each week. As a result, after week two, I increased the number of reps and weights at appropriate stations to make the circuit more demanding. I continued to use progressive overload by increasing the number of reps and weights every two weeks or so. As a result, my hand strength improved, from 25 to 30 (Appendix 2); this is at the top end of average compared to national hand strength norms. This increase has helped me to produce more power in my golf swing along with my good natural club head speed.

Heart rate

Over the duration of my PEP, my resting heart rate decreased by 6 b.p.m. (Appendix 3), while I was able to increase my working heart rate to 115 b.p.m., an improvement of 12 b.p.m.. Also my recovery time after exercise decreased from 18 minutes to 15 minutes. This indicates that my heart became more **efficient** and as a result my cardiovascular fitness improved.

Training methods

The method of training I used in my PEP were clearly effective as it caused the adaptations I needed to improve my power and achieve the targets I had set for myself. I really enjoyed the circuit training, which also worked well as I was able to increase the strength of my muscles, making me stronger and therefore helping me to increase my driving distance.

SMART targets

It is clear from my results that my targets were SMART as I have been successful in achieving one of them and making progress on the other in the realistic eight-week time frame I had planned for. To increase intensity and to provide **motivation**, I also set weekly targets; I increased reps and weights as the weeks passed in accordance with how I felt. These targets were easily measurable and by comparing to previous weeks I was able to calculate that, on the whole, I was successful in achieving these motivating short-term targets.

Principles of training

I began my PEP by setting what I thought was an appropriate number of reps, **sets** and weights to complete in each training session. I found after the first week that the training sessions were too easy, so I increased the intensity for the following week. Then, to ensure **progressive overload**, I increased the intensity of my circuit training every couple of weeks. This increase of intensity was based on my session measurements and how I felt at the end of each session. I had to be careful not to increase the intensity too much in order to avoid injury, but at the same time, I had to keep the sessions challenging and enjoyable to avoid demotivation. Luckily I avoided any injuries, which I believe was due to careful monitoring of my weekly performances, how I felt at the end of each session and my effective warm-ups and cool-downs. This progressive overload helped me to increase my power helping me to achieve my golf fitness component targets.

> Start by looking at post-PEP fitness data and make comparisons between your fitness levels before and after completing your PEP.

Appendix 1:

Target	Pre-PEP	Target	Post-PEP
Drive distance (average)	230 metres	245 metres	250 metres
Handicap	16	14	15

Appendix 2:

Fitness component	Test	Pre-PEP	Target	Post-PEP
Strength	Grip dynamometer test	25	28	30

Pre- and post-PEP results:

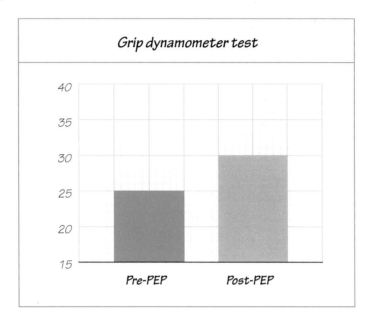

Appendix 3:

	Pre-PEP	Target	Post-PEP
Resting heart rate	75 b.p.m.	70 b.p.m.	69 b.p.m.
Working heart rate	103 b.p.m.	113 b.p.m.	115 b.p.m.
Recovery rate	18 minutes	16 minutes	15 minutes

Have a go!

Now that you have seen an example evaluation for a young golfer and developed a knowledge and understanding of the important information you need to include, you are now ready to write an evaluation from the following set of results for a hockey player.

This hockey player followed this eight-week training programme.

	Monday	**Tuesday (circuits)**	**Wednesday**	**Thursday (circuits)**	**Friday**
Week 1	Cooper's 12-minute run test	2 × 30 seconds	Game	2 × 30 seconds	Rest
Week 2	Rest	2 × 30 seconds	Game	2 × 30 seconds	Rest
Week 3	Rest	2 × 40 seconds	Game	2 × 40 seconds	Rest
Week 4	Cooper's 12-minute run test	2 × 40 seconds	Game	2 × 40 seconds	Rest
Week 5	Rest	2 × 50 seconds	Game	2 × 50 seconds	Rest
Week 6	Rest	2 × 50 seconds	Game	2 × 50 seconds	Rest
Week 7	Rest	2 × 60 seconds	Game	2 × 60 seconds	Rest
Week 8	Cooper's 12-minute run test	2 × 60 seconds	Game	2 × 60 seconds	Rest

Test results:

The results are for a sports person who plays midfield in the U16 hockey team, so it is important that they can beat players to the ball, intercept passes and maintain their performance for a complete match. Cardiovascular fitness is therefore very important to a hockey player playing in this position.

	Pre-PEP	**Target**	**Post-PEP**
Resting heart rate	75 b.p.m.	69 b.p.m.	67 b.p.m.
Working heart rate	102 b.p.m.	114 b.p.m.	114 b.p.m.
Recovery rate	17 minutes	15 minutes	14 minutes 30 seconds

Performance target	**Pre-PEP**	**Target**	**Post-PEP**
Number of interceptions	10	15	16

Fitness component	**Test**	**Pre-PEP**	**Target**	**Post-PEP**
Cardiovascular fitness	Cooper run	1650 m	1800 m	1950 m

To complete your evaluation, you must:

- Compare pre-, mid- and post-EP fitness and performance data.
- Analyse the changes specific to the focus activity.
- Draw valid and logical conclusions.
- Write a statement about the overall effectiveness of the PEP. You need to refer to evidence that supports the improvements in performance as well as fitness, or give reasons for why improvements did not take place.

You also need to write a statement about the following:

 i) Did the method of training improve the hockey player's performance, as well as their fitness?
 ii) Were the SMART targets achieved?
iii) Did they apply the principles of training appropriately?

Here are example tables that you can use for your evaluation to help you present your information.

Week number	Monday	Tuesday	Wednesday	Thursday	Friday

Test result			
	Pre-PEP	Target	Average
Resting heart rate			
Working heart rate			
Recovery rate			

Performance target	Pre-PEP	Target	Post-PEP

Fitness component	Test	Pre-PEP	Target	Post-PEP

See Appendix 3, p. 108 for the answers.

Exam-style questions

1. Below is the data recorded by a 15-year-old female during an eight-week training programme to improve her muscular endurance.

Body part	Exercise	Reps wk 1	Reps wk 4	Reps wk 8
Upper body	Sit ups	13	18	23
Upper body	Press ups	9	15	21
Lower body	Wall sit	25	32	41

Apply principles of training and methods of training, evaluate why the improvements in performance took place over the course of her fitness programme. (6)

....

....

....

....

....

....

....

....

....

....

....

....

2. The following data is for a 16-year-old male who undertook an eight-week training programme designed to improve his fitness. Evaluate why the changes took place. (6)

Component	Week 1	Week 8
Cooper's 12-minute run test	2123 m	2654 m
% body fat	21	14
Resting heart rate	75 b.p.m.	67 b.p.m.

....

....

....

....

....

....

....

....

....

....

....

....

....

revisit ◄*reflect* ►*revise!*

- **Revisit** the work completed so far in your PEP.
- **Reflect** on your evaluation of the hockey player results. Did you make valid and logical conclusions regarding the player's progress in their performance, and whether or not they achieved their target? Did you compare their results to normative data? How have you used the data provided to support your conclusions?
- **Revise** any key words and look over the use of data topic in Component 2: Health and Performance to help you analyse and evaluate statistical data and interpret it against normative data in physical activity and sport.

Now that you've had a go, assess your work against the criteria and consider the following:

- Based on the content of your work, what level would you place your work at?
- Look back over your work, what do you need to get to the next level?

Remember you're trying to achieve the top level.

WHAT'S MY LEVEL?

Edexcel: level descriptors for post-PEP analysis and evaluation

Edexcel

Level 1	Level 2	Level 3	Level 4	Level 5
Limited comparison, interpretation and/or analysis of differences and/or similarities between fitness test results and little/no supporting evidence used, with many significant errors of judgement/inaccuracies. Limited evaluation of the application of the method(s) of training, SMART goals and principles of training, and no recommendation for improving future training and performance.	Attempts to compare and interpret the fitness test results, with some differences and/or similarities analysed in places and some supporting evidence used, but with many errors of judgement/inaccuracies. Some attempts at evaluation of the application of the method(s) of training, SMART goals and principles of training, with some attempt at recommendation for improving future training and performance, but with significant errors.	Fitness test results are compared and interpreted, and the differences and/or similarities are analysed and sufficient supporting evidence used, but with some errors of judgement/inaccuracies. Good evaluation of the application of the method(s) of training, SMART goals and principles of training, with sufficient detail/depth, and appropriate recommendation(s) to improve future training and performance.	Fitness test results are compared and interpreted, and the differences and/or similarities are analysed with satisfactory supporting evidence, but with some minor errors of judgment/inaccuracies. Well-argued evaluation of the application of the method(s) of training, SMART goals and principles of training, in satisfactory detail and depth, with justified recommendations to improve future training and performance.	Fitness tests results are compared and interpreted, and the differences and/or similarities identified and analysed, and reasons for them justified, with ample supporting evidence. Sophisticated evaluation of the application of the method(s) of training, SMART goals and principles of training, in good detail and depth, with well justified recommendations to improve future training and performance.

This chapter focuses on the evaluation and application of the methods of training, SMART goals and principles of training elements of the post-PEP evaluation level descriptors.

Links to key areas

Below are recommended links to **Components 1** and **2**. Look over your class notes and apply to your PEP.

Component 1: Fitness and Body Systems

 Topic 3: Physical training (3.2)

 Topic 4: Use of data (4.1)

Component 2: Health and Performance

 Topic 2: Sports psychology (2.3)

 Topic 4: Use of data (4.1)

KEY WORDS

Adaptations	Evaluate	Normative data
Agility	Flexibility	Progressive overload
Cardiovascular fitness	Logical	Sets
Coordination	Motivation	Validity/valid
Correlation		

Evaluate performance: have you improved?

Hints and tips

- Your evaluation needs to focus on how successful your PEP was in achieving your stated targets.

- Make sure you state how your PEP brought about the desired improvements in your fitness and in particular the effect this had on your performances.

- Make sure that your pre- and post-PEP data is included in your evaluation.

- You need to analyse data and apply this to sporting examples and national norms.

- You only need to refer to the fitness test that relates to the component of fitness you have been working on.

- Have you applied theory to your conclusions?

7 Future performance

Now that you have completed the evaluation of your PEP, you now need to make recommendations on how you would further improve your level of fitness with the intention of continuing to improve your future performance in your chosen activity.

What to do and why

Discuss your results and your evaluation of your PEP with your teachers, parents, carers and coaches. Ensure that you identify the factors that had a *positive* effect on your performance and how you might develop these in the future. Make sure you also identify any factors that had a *negative* effect on your performance during your training programme and consider how you would overcome these in the future. Thinking about your plans, hopes and goals for the future (and based on the effectiveness of your PEP) make good clear **recommendations** on how to improve your future performances.

Figure 7.1 is the example profiling document that you met in Chapter 4. You can use this to guide discussions before, during and at the end of your PEP. This evidence can be used to help you make recommendations to bring about improvements in your chosen activity.

Identify the factors that might have a positive effect on your future performance

Coach/teacher pre-meeting notes:

....

....

....

....

Player pre-meeting notes:

....

....

....

....

Coach/teacher feedback:

....

....

....

....

....

Player feedback:

....

....

....

....

Recommendations for improvements:

....

....

....

....

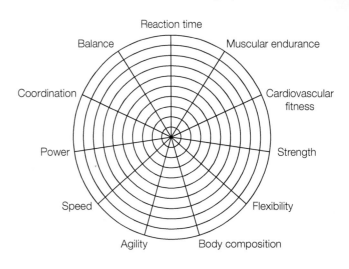

Coach/teacher radar graph

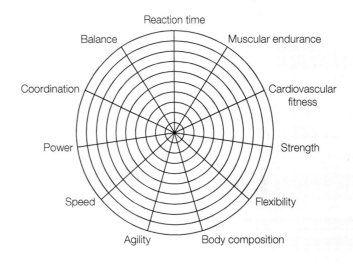

Performer's radar graph

Figure 7.1 Profiling document

How to do it

1. Discuss with teachers, parents, carers and coaches any results and information you have recorded in your training records, logbook, diary or profiling documents.
2. Based on your discussions and your evaluation of the effectiveness or ineffectiveness of your PEP, write a statement recommending how you would maintain, extend or improve your training programme in the future in order to ensure continued improvement in your sporting performance.
3. Thinking about aspects of your PEP that worked well and those that didn't work so well, state which type of training you would change and how you hope these changes would improve your future performance. Identify and justify any amendments to the methods and/or principles of training, thinking about variety and motivation and method of training reps/sets.

4. Identify any factors from the following list that affected your sporting performance or progress during your PEP and explain how they may affect your plans for your future performance:
    - time commitment and pressures
    - cost
    - facilities and their availability
    - injury
    - plateau of performance
    - motivation and relationships
    - diet.

5. State how you plan to overcome or avoid these in the future. Reflect on your targets and say whether they will need further development or change.

6. Finally, state how you will collect and use data in the future to bring about improved performance.

Example

Work/life balance

Cost

Plateau of performance

Motivation

Availability

Here is an extract from a PEP for a 16-year-old swimmer who wanted to improve their 1500 m time.

Swimming endurance

Overall my PEP was fairly effective and I felt that I worked hard during my training sessions. I showed improvements in my endurance swimming and I did manage to complete most of my short- and medium-term targets and part of my long-term goal. However, I didn't quite manage to reduce my 1500 m freestyle swim time enough and, therefore, did not achieve the main target I was aiming for. I think that was because I didn't have enough time to reach it due to the time I needed to revise for my exams.

Therefore, to extend or improve my training programme in the future to achieve the performance targets in my chosen activity, I would carry out my training plan over a longer period of time if I could find the time and money to do so. I would do this by adding an additional eight weeks to my training programme with the target of improving my 1500 m time if I can. During my anaerobic sessions in the swimming pool I will adjust my interval training by increasing the distance and number of repetitions in each swim set. I would plan to complete three workouts per week for the duration of my plan, resting every other day. I also plan to race for my local swimming team most Saturdays during this period. Some of the training would be in school and the rest at my local swimming pool if they could fit me in, with each session lasting 45 minutes.

Have a go!

Using the example of the swimmer on page 88, have a go at explaining how the following factors could affect the 16-year-old swimmer's future training plans. Make sure you give examples for each of the factors and how they would affect their training programme and therefore their sporting performance:

- work/life balance
- time commitment and pressures
- cost
- facilities and their availability
- injury
- plateau of performance
- motivation and relationships
- diet

For example, work/life balance: *'Studying for exams is reducing my training opportunities'* and then link to your swimming plan. *'I've had to reduce the number of my training sessions per week in order to give me more time to revise'.*

Exam-style questions

1. Describe the methods a coach could use to motivate a sportsperson to improve his/her performance. (5)

See Appendix 3, p.108 for the answers.

Remember that writing explanations, rather than just lists, gives you more marks.

2. Discuss why is it important that an athlete has variety in their training. (4)

....

....

....

....

....

....

....

....

....

....

revisit ◄ reflect ► revise!

- **Revisit** your evaluation in Chapter 6, checking against your recommendations to improve your future performance.
- **Reflect** on how you have applied theory, including knowledge of principles of training, method of training, reps/sets, energy systems, training zones, use of technology, analysing data and application to sporting examples.
- **Revise** the key words.

Now that you've had a go, assess your work against the criteria and consider the following:

- Based on the content of your work, what level would you place your work at?
- Look back over your work. What do you need to get to the next level?

Remember you're trying to achieve the top level.

WHAT'S MY LEVEL?

Edexcel: level descriptors for post-PEP evaluation

Edexcel

Level 1	Level 2	Level 3	Level 4	Level 5
Limited evaluation of the application of the method(s) of training, SMART goals and principles of training, and no recommendation for improving future training and performance.	Some attempts at evaluation of the application of the method(s) of training, SMART goals and principles of training, with some attempt at recommendation for improving future training and performance, but with significant errors.	Good evaluation of the application of the method(s) of training, SMART goals and principles of training, with sufficient detail/depth, and appropriate recommendation(s) to improve future training and performance.	Well-argued evaluation of the application of the method(s) of training, SMART goals and principles of training, in satisfactory detail and depth, with justified recommendations to improve future training and performance.	Sophisticated evaluation of the application of the method(s) of training, SMART goals and principles of training, in good detail and depth, with well justified recommendations to improve future training and performance.

This chapter focuses on the recommendations to improve future training and performance elements of the post-PEP evaluation level descriptors.

Links to key areas

Below are recommended links to **Components 1** and **2**. Look over your class notes and apply to your PEP.

Component 2: Health and Performance

 Topic 1: Health, fitness and wellbeing (1.1)

 Topic 2: Sports psychology (2.2 & 2.3)

 Topic 3: Socio-cultural influences (3.1)

Hints and tips

- Have you applied theory and shown your knowledge of principles of training, methods of training and application to sporting examples?

- Make sure you check your recommendations by comparing them with the required level descriptors for the specification.

- Make sure you explain how you hope your recommendations will *improve your future performance* in your chosen sport and not just how you would change your training programme.

KEY WORD

Recommendation

In this chapter you will produce the final written evaluation of your PEP and explain how it will help to improve fitness and performance in your chosen activity. This chapter will guide you through the process, so you can create a final structured, clear and informative PEP.

> Anything you put in your appendices will not be marked, so only include information in them that *supports* your analysis or evaluations from the main body of your submission.

What to do and why

Your PEP needs to use appropriate content, detail and the correct terminology throughout. If you wish to include any other evidence or information to support your PEP, it can be put in an appendix, but make sure you refer to these in the main body of your submission. Make sure you cover the following **objectives** and assessment **criteria**.

> Edexcel

Edexcel objectives

The following objectives have been paraphrased and restructured from the Edexcel GCSE (9–1) Physical Education specification document:

1. Initial analysis – Interpretation and analysis of pre-PEP fitness tests and sporting/activity performance
2. Initial evaluation – Evaluation and justification of method(s) of training, SMART targets and principles of training
3. Post-PEP analysis – Fitness test results are compared and interpreted
4. Post-PEP evaluation – Evaluation of the overall effectiveness of your PEP in improving performance, including evaluation of the application of the method(s) of training, SMART targets and principles of training with justified future recommendations
5. Overall coherence and structure – Use of appropriate terminology

Edexcel assessment criteria

Objectives	Level 1 (1–4 marks)	Level 2 (5–8 marks)	Level 3 (9–12 marks)	Level 4 (13–16 marks)	Level 5 (17–20 marks)
Initial analysis	Limited or little interpretation of fitness test results using some data.	Some attempt at interpretation and analysis of fitness test results using some data, but with errors that may impact analysis.	Good interpretation and analysis of fitness test results using appropriate data, with some errors that have insignificant impact on the analysis.	Very good interpretation and analysis of fitness test results using appropriate data, with one or two minor errors not significantly affecting the analysis.	Excellent and thorough interpretation and analysis of fitness test results using appropriate data.

Objectives	Level 1 (1–4 marks)	Level 2 (5–8 marks)	Level 3 (9–12 marks)	Level 4 (13–16 marks)	Level 5 (17–20 marks)
Initial evaluation	Limited evaluation (mainly descriptive) resulting in inappropriate selection of training method(s) and little application of SMART targets and principles of training to meet performance goal(s).	Some attempts at evaluation, with weak justification for training method(s) chosen, and attempts at applying SMART targets and principles of training to meet performance goal(s), with errors of judgement affecting the quality of the evaluation.	Good evaluation with appropriate training method(s) selected and explained, and application of SMART targets and principles of training to meet performance goal(s), with some errors of judgement that have insignificant impact on the evaluation.	Evaluation with appropriate training method(s) selected and explained, and application of SMART targets and principles of training to meet performance goal(s), with few errors of judgement not significantly affecting the evaluation.	Evaluation with appropriate training method(s) selected and justified, and application of SMART targets and principles of training to meet performance goal(s).
Post-PEP analysis	Limited comparison, interpretation and/ or analysis of differences and/ or similarities between fitness test results and little/no supporting evidence used, with many significant errors of judgement/ inaccuracies.	Attempts to compare and interpret the fitness test results, with some differences and/or similarities analysed in places and some supporting evidence used, but with many errors of judgement/ inaccuracies.	Fitness test results are compared and interpreted, and the differences and/or similarities are analysed and sufficient supporting evidence used, but with some errors of judgement/ inaccuracies.	Fitness test results are compared and interpreted, and the differences and/or similarities are analysed with satisfactory supporting evidence, but with some minor errors of judgment/ inaccuracies.	Fitness tests results are compared and interpreted, and the differences and/or similarities identified and analysed, and reasons for them justified, with ample supporting evidence.
Post-PEP evaluation	Limited evaluation of the application of the method(s) of training, SMART goals and principles of training, and no recommendation for improving future training and performance.	Some attempts at evaluation of the application of the method(s) of training, SMART goals and principles of training, with some attempt at recommendation for improving future training and performance, but with significant errors.	Good evaluation of the application of the method(s) of training, SMART goals and principles of training, with sufficient detail/depth, and appropriate recommendation(s) to improve future training and performance.	Well-argued evaluation of the application of the method(s) of training, SMART goals and principles of training, in satisfactory detail and depth, with justified recommendations to improve future training and performance.	Sophisticated evaluation of the application of the method(s) of training, SMART goals and principles of training, in good detail and depth, with well justified recommendations to improve future training and performance.
Overall coherence and conciseness of the student's PEP	Lack of coherence and structure, with inappropriate and inaccurate terminology throughout.	Attempts at coherence and structure, with use of appropriate terminology in places but inconsistent and with some errors of judgement.	Good coherence and structure, with appropriate terminology used, but some errors of judgement/accuracy with no significant impact on the piece.	Very good coherence and structure, with appropriate terminology used throughout, but with a few minor errors.	Excellent coherence and structure, with appropriate terminology used consistently, with few minor, if any, errors.

How to do it

- Make sure your PEP is well structured, clear and concise and takes an evaluative approach that enables you to access all the assessment levels.
- It is very important that you make the connection between the exercise programme and your performance.
- Ensure that you focus on the effectiveness of your PEP in bringing about your stated target and, more importantly, how this impacted on your performance.

Consider this outline as one way of structuring your work. Your teacher may have other approaches you may wish to think about too.

Initial analysis

1. **Introduction**: Identify your chosen sport/activity and include background information about yourself as a performer, your age and your experience.
2. **Interpretation and analysis of current fitness levels**: Compare your current performance measures against normative data, include fitness testing and protocols, components of fitness specific to the sport and position or activity. Include evaluation of your performance measures, identifying strengths and weaknesses and areas for improvement.

Initial evaluation

3. **Recommendations to improve fitness and performance in the chosen activity**: Referencing the component of fitness you wish to address describe the **recommendation** to develop fitness to bring about improvements in performance. Evaluate and justify methods of training, SMART targets and principles of training.
4. **A plan of the exercise programme**: Outline your training plan including duration of programme, how many sessions, with evidence of principles of training and method of training and intensities of training. Remember your plan should be placed in an appendix but data included should be referenced in your evaluation where appropriate.
5. **Completing and monitoring the programme**: Details of how you carried out your training plan, how you monitored it and how you collected data (including any changes you made while you carried it out).

Post-PEP analysis/evaluation

6. **Evaluation of the programme**: Make sure that fitness test results are compared and interpreted. Use data collected so you can evaluate the effectiveness of your programme and any improvements, as well as the impact it had on your performance. Ensure you evaluate your use of principles of training, method of training and the effect that having SMART targets had on your training and performance.
7. **Recommendations for improvements to personal performance in the chosen activity**: Recommend ways to improve your training for future improvement in your personal performance and how you could extend, challenge and/or change your plan. Make sure you refer to any factors that could affect your future plans and discuss the impact on your fitness and sporting performance.

Hints and tips

Throughout your written submission think about your use of the following:

- Structure
- Spelling, punctuation and grammar
- Presentation
- Use of text, diagrams, graphs, tables, photographs, etc.

Task

Read through the following examples that cover the objectives required for a PEP. The examples are for different students covering a variety of sports.

Assess the following against the assessment criteria, p. 6–7, and give suggestions on how these examples could meet the top level.

Initial analysis

Is the initial analysis detailed?

Are there comparisons to normative data?

Applied theory

Have they applied theoretical content?

How could they link discussion to planning an exercise programme?

Example

Example 1

Introduction and initial analysis: Swimmer

I am 16 years old and have swum since I was eight years old. My main achievements are that I have represented my local swimming club as well as my school team. I am also currently training to swim the 1500 m in the county championships in the hope that I can go further to reach a higher level of competition.

My normative data (Appendix 1) shows that my strengths are speed and power, but that my cardiovascular fitness is not as good as it should be. My coach's data (Appendix 2) highlights this weakness as they show that both my speed and power drop off towards the end of the race. My split times slow by up to two seconds per length demonstrating the need for me to develop my endurance to last the duration of a 1500 m swim.

Example 2

Recommendations to improve fitness and performance in the chosen activity: Hockey player

Component of fitness target: My target is to improve my agility.

My target is to improve my agility. This target is specific, as it is a key aspect of my performance as a midfielder in hockey and has been highlighted as one of my areas for improvement. Agility is useful in hockey to perform tackles, dribbling and intercepting passes. I will measure my improvement through conducting the Illinois agility run test at the beginning and end of an eight-week training programme. My coach also believes that improvement in this area will be beneficial, and I feel that realistically I should be aiming for a one-second improvement after the training programme.

I will improve my agility by using interval training, because it allows me to work at high intensity with rests, so I can focus on changing direction at speed.

Example 3

A plan of my exercise programme: Dancer

In my exercise programme, I am going to focus on one SMART target.

My circuit training is going to be specific to the component of fitness that I am trying to improve as I have included many stations that work on my muscular endurance. I've also included some dance style lunges to link my training programme to my sport. I am going to include lots of stations that will help me to improve the muscular endurance in my legs. I will measure my progress at four weeks and then at eight weeks. I am doing this so that I can see if my circuit is actually beneficial to me. To measure my progress, I will be re-doing the fitness tests which corresponds with my identified weakness. My coach and I decided on my target together. We did this so that we could both agree on what my weakness is so that we could discuss which stations to include.

I think that my target is realistic, because I will be training every week. I also attend dance lessons three times a week, so this will help me to improve my muscular endurance further. I will have eight weeks to complete my training programme.

Example 4

Completion and monitoring the programme: Athlete

*This morning, I felt prepared and **confident** about the upcoming circuit training session. My mood was fairly good and I was relatively happy. I felt prepared to go through the training session and knew that I was going to be able to perform with quite a lot of effort. Considering all of the factors above, I believe that my session was successful and I believe that I performed better this week than in the previous two weeks.*

RPE is short for '**rate of perceived exertion**'.

My average work rate was 30 seconds on and then 30 seconds rest, but two stations were 40 seconds on and 20 seconds off. During the upcoming weeks, I am planning on increasing the work time for every station with my end goal being one minute work, 30 seconds rest. This week my RPE ranged from 12–16. This implies that this circuit was the most challenging out of the three weeks I have completed. Personally, I found the crunches the most challenging to complete, as I have increased the work time and decreased the rest time for that station. I feel as though I worked the hardest on this station, purely because the work time was the highest. The exercise I found the easiest was the plank. I know this as my RPE was a 12; I think I found this the easiest because I am quite used to performing a plank and have always found them quite easy to complete. Next week, I am going to alter two of my stations. I am going to overload the step-ups by increasing the work time to 40 seconds and sit-ups by adding a 5 kg weight to the exercise. I am going to leave all of my other stations the same and over the following weeks I will overload them.

Example 5

Evaluation of the programme: Basketball player

My post-PEP fitness results showed that I increased my vertical jump test from 30 to 38 cm, which was 1 cm more than my SMART target. This improvement corresponded to my increased percentage of rebounds during matches, which means these aims were realistic and achievable. I believe that the success of my PEP was due to planning my training sessions with principles of training in mind, making them specific to my sport of basketball. I included stations in my circuit with similar movements to those used while playing basketball, such as passing and shooting; I also ensured the intensity of the interval training matched the intensity that I experience during game play and therefore made the training relevant to basketball. I used progressive overload in my circuits by increasing the number of repetitions at each station appropriate to my weekly fitness level. This progressive overload made the sessions sufficiently challenging, which helped build the power in my legs.

Example 6

Recommendations for improvements to personal performance in the chosen activity: Swimmer

To improve my PEP, I would begin by collecting a baseline for my swimming times in races. Then at the interim stage, I would test my swim times again. The reason I would do this is I believe it would have a greater impact on my motivation and therefore my effort levels in training, which would impact my overall performance. I would also consider adding another method of training to my programme such as plyometrics, as this would have a big impact on my power. Improving my power even more would have a strong impact on my dive and my turns, improving my race times particularly on a 25 m course. The only part that I didn't like about my programme was that we were not able to do it more times a week. The changes that I would make would be to make it a bit longer (to fully see the results and have a larger impact on my performance) and to find a closer gym (or use one in the school) because we did not have very much time to work out when we got there due to time spent travelling.

Have a go!

Now it is time for you to complete your PEP. Follow the structure outlined in the 'How to do it' earlier in this chapter (p.94), and refer to the examples on pages 95 to 97. This will help you ensure your PEP is well structured, clear, informative and meets the required criteria. Remember that the examples on how to write your PEP are just that. To achieve top marks you will need to give more thorough interpretation, analysis, justification in each section of your evaluation.

You will be required to submit your PEP in one of two formats: written or verbal.

Written PEP:

The written version should have a **maximum of 1500 words**. You will only be assessed on the analysis and evaluation of your written words. Any PARQ forms, graphs, charts, tables, diagrams/flow charts, and training record forms do not count towards your word count. Training record forms for each training session (or appropriate alternative evidence) must be submitted and may be presented as an appendix to your PEP.

Verbal presentation:

This is submitted via video evidence with a maximum presenting time of 15 minutes. You will be assessed on your verbal analysis and evaluation of your PEP. You may use presenting tools (e.g. presentation software and/or cue cards) but this is optional. Training record forms for each training session (or appropriate alternative evidence) must be submitted. Any presentation slides used must also be submitted.

Good luck!

> Remember, you will be assessed only on the analysis and evaluation of your PEP and how it impacted on your sporting performance. You are not assessed on whether or not any improvement occurs in your performance, or on the actual carrying out of your PEP.

Exam-style questions

1. As a GCSE student you will have followed a personal exercise programme. Evaluate, using examples, how you have applied the principles of training to your personal exercise programme. (7)

....

....

....

....

....

(blank lined box)

revisit ◀ reflect ▶ revise!

- **Revisit** your PEP and do a self-assessment as to where you think it would be placed on the assessment grid. Then go back and improve your PEP to get it to the next level.
- **Reflect** on the connections between your PEP and the theory you learnt during the introduction to physical education element of your GCSE PE course, so you consolidate your learning.
- **Revise** key words.

Now that you've had a go, assess your work against the criteria and consider the following:

- Based on the content of your work, what level would you place your work at?
- Look back over your work. What do you need to get to the next level?

Remember you're trying to achieve the top level.

WHAT'S MY LEVEL?

Edexcel: level descriptors for overall coherence and conciseness of the student's PEP

Edexcel

Level 1	Level 2	Level 3	Level 4	Level 5
Lack of coherence and structure, with inappropriate and inaccurate terminology throughout.	Attempts at coherence and structure, with use of appropriate terminology in places but inconsistent and with some errors of judgement.	Good coherence and structure, with appropriate terminology used, but some errors of judgement/ accuracy with no significant impact on the piece.	Very good coherence and structure, with appropriate terminology used throughout, but with a few minor errors.	Excellent coherence and structure, with appropriate terminology used consistently, with few minor, if any, errors.

Hints and tips

- Read your final PEP aloud to a friend.
- Get a parent/guardian/coach to read it and ask questions.
- Refer to the level descriptors – aim for the top level.

Criteria

Objectives

Rate of perceived exertion (RPE)

Recommendation

Links to key areas

Below are recommended links to **Components 1** and **2**. Look over your class notes and apply to your PEP.

Component 1: Fitness and Body Systems

 Topic 4: Use of data (4.1)

Component 2: Health and Performance

 Topic 4: Use of data (4.1)

Glossary

Abdominal muscle A large group of muscles in the front of the abdomen that aid regular breathing movement and support the muscles of the spine.

Adaptable Adjust to new conditions.

Adaptations Changes to meet the needs, interests, and abilities of each individual.

Adherence The act of doing something according to a particular standard or agreement.

Aerobic 'With oxygen'. Type of physical activity that uses large muscle groups and can be sustained for at least 10 minutes (e.g. walking and jogging).

Aerobic target zone The aerobic target zone is the intensity at which your body is using aerobic metabolism (60–80% of maximum heart rate).

Aesthetic Natural body movement and feeling when performing.

Agility The ability to change the position of the body quickly and to control the movement of the whole body.

Anaerobic 'Without oxygen'. Exercise that causes you to be quickly out of breath, like sprinting or lifting a heavy weight.

Anaerobic threshold (AT) The point during exercise when your body must switch from aerobic to anaerobic metabolism.

Anaerobic target zone Fuelled by glycogen and carbohydrates rather than oxygen (80%+ of maximum heart rate).

Balance Stability of the body's centre of mass over a base of support with reference to static (stationary), or dynamic (changing), conditions of movement, shape and orientation.

Blood pressure (BP) The force exerted by circulating blood on the walls of the blood vessels. Expressed as two numbers; the top number is systolic and the bottom number diastolic (e.g. 120/80).

Body composition The percentage of body weight that is fat, muscle and bone.

Cardiovascular fitness (aerobic endurance) The ability to exercise the entire body for long periods of time.

Cardiovascular system The circulatory system consisting of the heart, arteries, capillaries and veins.

Characteristics The features or qualities belonging to a person or thing.

Components of fitness Elements of exercise and fitness specific to the needs of the individual and demands of the activity.

Confident Feeling certain or showing certainty about something.

Control To have control is to have power to run something in an orderly way. In sport, control can be both emotional and physical.

Controlled To run or perform something in an orderly way.

Coordination The ability to combine movements of two or more body parts at the same time.

Correlation How closely two related sets of data are linked.

Criteria A standard on which a judgement or decision may be based.

Diastolic blood pressure The time in the cardiac cycle when the heart refills with blood.

Duration Length of time you exercise for.

Dynamic stretching Form of active movement that isn't about holding a stretch but rather taking your body through ranges of motion that will better prepare you for your workout or sporting activity.

Efficient Perform with minimum wasted effort.

Evaluate Measuring and judging the effectiveness, outcomes, or quality of an activity or programme.

Failure The point where you can no longer continue.

Fartlek training A continuous form of training with changes in speed and terrain to provide changes in exercise intensity.

Field tests Performed on the sports field or in a sports hall. They tend to be basic in nature and do not need specialist equipment.

Fitness Meeting the demands of the environment.

FITT Frequency, intensity, time, type (used to increase the amount of work the body does in order to achieve overload).

Flexibility The range of movements possible at a joint.

Fluency To express movement easily and articulately.

Frequency How often you exercise.

Gluteus maximus The largest of the muscles that are located in the buttock.

Goals Targets set to provide focus.

Health A state of physical, mental and social wellbeing with the absence of disease.

Heart rate (HR) The number of times the heart beats each minute.

Intensity How hard you work during exercise.

Isometric stretching A way of stretching to increase flexibility (held for up to 30 seconds, using correct technique).

Laboratory tests Performed in sport and exercise laboratories and generally using specialist equipment.

Lactic acid system The lactic acid system uses stored glucose to create energy.

Ligaments Short bands of tough, flexible, fibrous tissue that connect many of the bones in the body together.

Logical A sensible decision when all the facts have been considered.

Maximal force The maximum energy your muscles can create.

Motivation Your drive to succeed and desire to achieve something.

Muscular endurance Ability to exercise a specific muscle group repeatedly over a period of time.

Muscular strength The amount of force a muscle can exert against a resistance.

National norms Published norms based around the averages and range of scores around the mean. Comparing your test scores against national norms will give you a rating and an indication of how you have performed in comparison to the general population.

Normative data After every test you measure not only against your own previous scores but also against national normative data. You can evaluate how you compare on a larger scale and whether or not you are improving.

Objective An aim or goal with a focus on outcomes.

Overload Increasing the frequency, intensity and duration of the method of training within the programme. Fitness can only be improved through training more than you normally do.

Physical Activity Readiness Questionnaire (PARQ) A questionnaire used as a method of uncovering health and lifestyle issues before taking part in physical activity.

Plyometric/s Exercises in which muscles exert maximum force in short intervals of time, with the goal of increasing power (strength × speed).

Power The ability to do strength performances quickly (power = strength × speed).

Principles of training A set of rules making training work for an individual.

Progression Where training is increased gradually as the body adjusts to the increased demands being made on it.

Progressive overload To gradually increase the amount of overload so that fitness gains occur, but without potential for injury

Proprioceptive neuromuscular facilitation (PNF) A form of stretching that increases the flexibility of muscles and improves range of movement.

Quadriceps The large muscle at the front of the thigh.

Rate of perceived exertion (RPE) A way of measuring exercise intensity.

Reaction time The time between the presentation of a stimulus and the onset of a movement.

Recommendation A suggestion or proposal as to the best course of action.

Reliability/Reliable Being dependably accurate and consistent.

Reps The number of times you perform an exercise.

Sets The number of times you repeat a particular exercise.

Shuttles Moving between two points.

Skilled performer Consistent, confident, effective, controlled and aesthetic.

SMART target A goal setting strategy (*Specific, Measurable, Achievable, Realistic and Time-bound*).

Specificity Matching training to the to the requirements of an activity.

Speed The ability to get from A to B as quickly as possible.

Systolic blood pressure The pressure when the heart pushes blood out.

Technical If someone is technical their movements have purpose, direction and produce a positive result.

Tendons A flexible but inelastic cord of strong tissue attaching a muscle to a bone.

Test protocols The official procedure outlining requirements, activity and resources.

Training zones The upper and lower limits of training intensities.

Triceps A large muscle on the back of the upper arm principally responsible for extension of the elbow joint (straightening of the arm).

Valid Using the correct test for the component of fitness.

Validity The extent to which a test or method measures what it sets out to measure.

Variance Changes of intensity, duration and volume while exercising.

Appendix 1: GCSE example checklist for your personal exercise programme

Appendix 1.1: Table checklist to monitor and track your progress

	Wk 1		Wk 2		Wk 3		Wk 4		Wk 5		Wk 6		Wk 7		Wk 8	
Sessions	1	2	3	4	5	6	7	8	9	10	11	12	13	14	15	16
Circuit completed																
Results recorded																
Logbook/diary/training record form done																
Performance factor measured																
Match played																

Appendix 1.2: Checklist to monitor tasks associated with completing your PEP

☐ Make sure you keep a record in your progress table, training record form, logbook or diary for all sessions that you complete.

☐ Have a review discussion after each training session. Talk about how it went, what you think about your level of fitness and how easy or difficult you found the session.

☐ Your records should describe how you feel and how closely training sessions match your plans, e.g. make comments on your post-exercise heart rate to help you monitor how hard you worked in the session.

☐ Follow your training programme for two or three weeks.

☐ At this point, collect performance data for your key target to see if you are making progress towards improving it.

☐ Carry out mid-point testing.

☐ If needed, make changes to your plan if you think this would help to improve the chances of you achieving your SMART targets.

☐ Continue with your updated plan for another two or three weeks.

☐ Evaluate and test again.

☐ Make further changes if required.

☐ Complete your updated training plan.

Appendix 2: GCSE Physical Education activity list

The activity list for the Edexcel specification can be found below.

Appendix 2.1: Edexcel GCSE Physical Education activity list

Edexcel

Team activities	
Activity	**Forbidden combinations and rules**
Acrobatic gymnastics*	
Association football	Cannot be five-a-side
Badminton	Cannot be assessed with singles/individual activity badminton
Basketball	Cannot be 'street basketball'
Camogie	Cannot be assessed with hurling
Cricket	
Dance	Acceptable dances include: ballet, ballroom, contemporary/modern, cultural (includes hip-hop, Irish, Indian, jazz, Latin), folk and street This can only be used for one activity
Field hockey	
Figure skating*	
Futsal*	
Gaelic football	
Handball	
Hurling	Cannot be assessed with camogie
Ice hockey*	
Inline/Roller hockey*	
Lacrosse	
Netball	
Rowing	Cannot be assessed with sculling, canoeing, kayaking or a rowing machine. This can only be used for one activity
Rugby league	Cannot be assessed with rugby union or rugby sevens; cannot be tag rugby
Rugby union	Can be assessed as sevens or fifteen-a-side. Cannot be assessed with rugby league; cannot be tag rugby. This can only be used for one activity
Sailing*	Cannot be assessed with singles/individual activity sailing. Royal Yachting Association recognised sailing-boat classes only. Students must perform as helmsman

Team activities	
Activity	Forbidden combinations and rules
Sculling*	Cannot be assessed with canoeing, kayaking or rowing
Squash	Cannot be assessed with singles/individual activity squash
Table tennis	Cannot be assessed with singles/individual activity table tennis
Tennis	Cannot be assessed with singles/individual activity tennis
Volleyball	
Water polo*	

Specialist activity**	
Blind cricket	
Goalball	
Powerchair football	
Table cricket	
Wheelchair basketball	
Wheelchair rugby	

Individual activities	
Activity	Forbidden combinations and rules
Amateur boxing	
Athletics	Can be assessed in one event from the disciplines of either track or field (including cross country*) Race walking is not a permitted athletics event
Badminton	Cannot be assessed with doubles
BMX cycling*	Racing only, not tricks
Canoeing	Cannot be assessed with kayaking, rowing or sculling
Cycling	Track or road cycling
Dance	This can only be used for one activity
Diving	Platform diving
Figure skating*	
Golf	
Gymnastics	Floor routines and apparatus
Equestrian	Can be assessed in either show jumping, cross country or dressage
Kayaking	Cannot be assessed with canoeing, rowing or sculling
Rock climbing	Can be indoor or outdoor
Sailing*	Cannot be assessed with sailing as a team activity. Royal Yachting Association recognised sailing-boat classes only
Sculling	Cannot be assessed with rowing, canoeing or kayaking
Skiing	Outdoor/indoor on snow. Cannot be assessed with snowboarding. Must not be on dry slopes
Snowboarding	Outdoor/indoor on snow. Cannot be assessed with skiing. Must not be on dry slopes

Individual activities	
Activity	**Forbidden combinations and rules**
Squash	Cannot be assessed with doubles
Swimming	Not synchronised swimming
Table tennis	Cannot be assessed with doubles
Tennis	Cannot be assessed with doubles
Trampolining	
Windsurfing*	
Specialist activity**	
Boccia	
Polybat	

*These activities are available for first teaching from September 2020 and first certification from Summer 2022.

**The specialist activities are available only to those students with a physical disability, and in line with entry criteria set out by that activity's National Governing Body.

If a student is classified as eligible, then they should be assessed in the classification based on the relevant activity's National Governing Body classification criteria.

Appendix 3: Answers to exam-style questions

Chapter 1

Question number	Answer	Mark
1	(AO1 – 1 mark) *One of:* income, gender, role models, peer pressure	(1)
2	(AO1 – 1 mark) *One of:* peers, coach, family, success, emotions, role models, etc.	(1)
3	(AO1 – 4 marks) *Four of:* technically sound, efficient, accurate, controlled, consistent, fluent	(4)
4	(AO1 – 1 marks) *Four of:* balance, cardiovascular fitness, coordination, strength, speed, body composition, agility, muscular endurance, reaction time, power, flexibility.	(4)

Note: There are no exam-style questions in Chapter 2.

Chapter 3

Question number	Answer	Mark
1	(AO1 – 2 marks) 20 m course, stay in time with the beeps on each line, run until exhaustion, three failed attempts end of test.	(2)
2	(AO1 – 1 mark) The ability to use strength at speed.	(1)
3	(AO1 – 1 mark) Vertical jump or standing broad jump.	(1)
4	(AO2 – 2 marks) **Validity** is using the correct test for the chosen component of fitness. **Reliability** is when the result is accurate and consistent.	(2)
5	(AO1 – 2 marks) (AO2 – 1 mark) Any *two* from: cardiovascular fitness, muscular endurance, power, strength, body composition; with an explanation for how they would be used to be effective in the game.	(3)

Chapter 4

Question number	Answer	Mark
1	(AO1 – 1 mark) Specific, Measurable, Achievable, Realistic, Time-bound	(1)
2	(AO2 – 1 mark) Targets help to focus attention and are critical to maintaining motivation.	(1)

Question number	Answer	Mark
3	(A01 – 2 marks) (A02 – 4 marks) Identifying SMART (1) Amplification (1) Explaining how SMART targets link to improving performance (3–4 marks): • Enabling success • Recognises progress • Motivation • Measurable/recorded • Control over what happens • Identifying challenges • Adherence.	**(6)**
4	(A02 – 1 mark) To reduce their times by two hundredths of a second or equivalent.	**(1)**
5	(A02 – 1 mark) The targets will have been discussed, shared and accepted.	**(1)**

Chapter 5

Question number	Answer	Mark
1	(A03 – 6 marks) As this is an evaluation question marks with only be given for the evaluation of: • the effects of monitoring on an athlete's motivation. • timing of monitoring to maintain motivation. • the purpose of monitoring. It should not focus on temporary changes and instead measure longer-term progress. • establishing an accurate baseline measure. • the importance of validity and reliability in tester monitoring. • the importance of comparisons with national norms.	**(6)**
2	(A01 – 2 marks) Any *two* of: • Equipment is not expensive / no specialist equipment is required • All levels can be accommodated/can be tailored to individual needs • Can be used with large groups • Can focus on any component of fitness • Can include both aerobic and anaerobic activities • Can include a wide variety of exercises to prevent boredom and maintain interest.	**(2)**
3	(A02 – 4 marks) *One* mark for giving any of the following reasons (up to four marks): • It allows the participant and coach/teacher to identify strengths and weaknesses • Measures improvement, if any • Identifies a baseline • Enables personalised goals to be set • Aids self-motivation • Helps in the recovery from injury • Supports the coach/teacher in selection • Monitors success of training programme • Allows for adaptation to training patterns • Programmes can be tailored to an individual's needs.	**(4)**

Chapter 6

Question number	Answer	Mark
1 and 2	(AO3 – 6 marks for each question) The evaluations must link the changes in the performance and explain why the changes could have taken place. • Principles of training • Overload described in terms of FITT • Mention could be made of the type of training undertaken • Links may be made between diet and nutrition and progress being made in performance • Possible links also to motivation and adherence strategies • Physiological adaptations in the short- and long-term.	**(6)**

Chapter 7

Question number	Answer	Mark
1	(AO2 – 5 marks) Max 1–2 marks for list, 3–5 marks for an explanation (e.g. a coach could motivate a sportsperson by giving them clear and regular feedback so they know exactly what progress they are making to achieving their goals). • Praise and criticise • Set goals • Rewards: tangible/intangible • Increase intrinsic motivation, which is a better source of long-term motivation • Knowledge of performance • Knowledge of results • Feedback: timely, constructive, accurate, appropriate • Comparisons with norms/others/themselves.	**(5)**
2	(AO2 – 4 marks) Max 1–2 marks for list, 3–4 marks for an explanation (e.g. It is important to have variety in your training because it allows for your body to be challenged on a consistent basis and to therefore overcome a plateau). • Adherence • Enjoyable, interesting, reduces boredom • Motivation • Avoid plateauing – improves performance/fitness • Environment.	**(4)**

Chapter 8

Question number	Answer	Mark
1	(AO3 – 7 marks) Max 1–3 marks for a list, 4–7 marks for an explanation. Students must use the principles of training: • Individual needs • Specificity • Progressive overload • F.I.T.T. (frequency, intensity, time, type) • Rest and recovery • Reversibility • Thresholds of training	**(7)**

Appendix 4: PARQ example proforma

PEP

PARQ
Physical Activity Readiness Questionnaire

Objective

A Physical Activity Readiness Questionnaire or PARQ is a method of uncovering health and lifestyle issues prior to taking part in an exercise programme.

Guidance

Please answer all questions as accurately as possible.

Personal details

Name: ....

D.O.B.: .... Age: ....

Height: .... Weight: ....

Emergency contact number: ....

Emergency contact name: ....

Relationship of contact: ....

Your address: ....

....

Contact number: ....

Questions

Are you currently under a doctor's care?   YES ☐   NO ☐

If YES explain: ....

When was the last time you had a physical examination? ....

Do you take any medication on a regular basis?   YES ☐   NO ☐

If YES, please list medications and reasons for taking: ....

....

Have you recently been hospitalised?   YES ☐   NO ☐

If YES explain: ....

Do you smoke?	YES ☐	NO ☐	History of breathing or lung problems?	YES ☐	NO ☐
Are you pregnant?	YES ☐	NO ☐	Increased blood cholesterol?	YES ☐	NO ☐
Do you drink alcohol more than three times a week?	YES ☐	NO ☐	Describe any regular physical activity you take part in:		
Do you have:			....		
History of heart problems, chest pains?	YES ☐	NO ☐	....		
High blood pressure?	YES ☐	NO ☐	....		

All the information is true to the best of my knowledge.   NAME:

SIGNATURE:

Appendix 5: Edexcel PEP training record form

Pearson Edexcel Level 1/Level 2 GCSE (9–1) in Physical Education	1PE0/04
Centre name:	Centre number:
Candidate name:	Candidate number:
Chosen activity/sport:	
Chosen method of training:	
Date and number of training session:	

Pre-exercise heart rate before warm-up	Working heart rate	Immediate post-exercise heart rate

Recovery heart rate at the following intervals (b.p.m.)	1 min	2 min	3 min	4 min	5 min

Description of training session appropriate to the method of training, e.g. map of continuous training course, plan of circuit training session

Any adaptions or changes I have made to this training session and why

Source: Pearson Edexcel (Issue 3 2020) 'GCSE (9-1) Physical Education' London, Pearson Education Limited. p. 47 [Online].